Student Learning as Student Affairs Work: Responding to Our Imperative

Elizabeth J. Whitt
Editor

Library of Congress
Cataloging-in-Publication Data

Student learning as student affairs work : responding to our imperative / Elizabeth J. Whitt, editor.
    p   cm. – (NASPA monograph series ; 23)
    Includes bibliographical references (p. xiii)
    ISBN 0-931654-27-0
    1. student affairs services—United States. 2. College student development
       programs—United States. 3. Experiential learning—United States.
       I. Whitt, Elizabeth J. II. National Association of Student Personnel
       Administrators (U.S.) III. Series: NASPA monograph series; v.23
    LB2342.9.S79 1999
    376.1'97—dc21   99-20778
                                                   CIP

OTHER NASPA MONOGRAPH TITLES

Contents

Preface

Elizabeth J. Whitt

> *When a new dawn reveals a landscape dotted with obstacles, the time*
> *has come for sober reflection, for assessment of our methods, and for*
> *anticipating pitfalls. Stumbling and groping through the wilderness*
> *finally must be replaced by a planned, organized and orderly march.*
> —Dr. Martin Luther King, Jr., *Where Do We*
> *Go From Here: Chaos or Community?* 1967

In the 1960s, Martin Luther King, Jr. urged his colleagues to reflect on the obstacles revealed by the new dawn of the civil rights movement, assess what they were doing and why, and plan for an orderly march toward achieving their goals. At the close of the 1990s, a "new dawn" of unprecedented change in higher education reveals to us a landscape similarly dotted with obstacles – or, as we prefer to talk about them here, challenges. These challenges include new students, new educational technologies and delivery systems, and new institutional structures and arrangements for conducting our work. At the same time, we must cope with shrinking financial resources and the fact that "public confidence in the 'people running higher education' has declined dramatically" (Wingspread Group, 1993, p. 6).

The Wingspread Group and other higher education reformers (e.g., NASULGC, 1997; Boyer Commission, 1998) have demanded that higher education address these challenges by focusing on the core function of colleges and universities: student learning. In 1993, Charles Schroeder, then president of the American College Personnel Association (ACPA), gathered student affairs scholars and practitioners together to consider the pressures and demands of this "new dawn" in higher education and their implications for student affairs practice. The result of their deliberations was the *Student Learning Imperative (SLI)* (1994), a strongly-worded challenge to our profession to direct our resources and efforts to facilitate student learning by creating "learning-oriented student affairs divisions."

The conversation about student learning and student affairs was expanded when Jon Dalton became president-elect of NASPA in 1994; he made the *SLI* and its implementation a priority for NASPA during his term of office. This emphasis on fostering student learning in student affairs took several forms within NASPA. Perhaps most important, the association's strategic plan (NASPA, 1995) includes the following goal: *to provide leadership for promoting, assessing, and supporting student learning and successful educational outcomes*. In addition, the theme of NASPA's 1996 conference — "When a new dawn reveals a landscape ... Redefining Learning" — drew the attention of participants to the challenges present in the landscape of American higher education and the need to redefine student affairs practice in terms of student learning.

Finally, President Dalton convened a team of student affairs professionals, faculty, and researchers — herein referred to as the Student Learning Project Work Group — to take an in-depth look at the implications of the *SLI* for student affairs work. What, for example, does the student affairs "landscape" – both outside and inside our institutions — look like? What does "student learning" mean in the context of student affairs work? How does student affairs contribute to student learning outcomes? How do we go about creating and maintaining learning-oriented student affairs divisions? This monograph is the result of our efforts.

K. Patricia Cross has noted that "those who reflect on their learning are better learners than those who do not" (Cross, 1994). Answering the questions just posed as a profession requires all of us to approach the "new dawn" as learners, reflecting on current obstacles, examining our current assumptions, beliefs, and practices, and planning a march into the future. To that end, we developed a set of questions and debatable "propositions" about the current landscape of student affairs work. The propositions formed the basis of several "reflection breaks" at the 1996 NASPA conference, and we offer them again here as a framework for thinking about our student learning imperative.

SOME DEBATABLE PROPOSITIONS

1. **In what ways must the student affairs landscape be altered to become more learning centered?**

   Proposition: Developing a learning orientation to student affairs work means a re-orientation of student affairs work: thinking of our work in terms of educational outcomes, such as critical thinking, moral reasoning, and appreciation for diversity, rather than as sets of activities, such as residence life, student activities, and judicial affairs. This means conducting different business — that is, actively seeking opportunities for student learning in everything we do — not doing the same business with different labels.

   Proposition: The classroom is the point of contact between most of today's students and their institutions; the classroom, therefore, is the locus of most teaching and learning. Out of class activities that do not relate directly to educational goals are, for the most part, not a productive use of our resources.

2. **In what ways do current student affairs assumptions, expectations, and practices inhibit student learning?**

   Proposition: Student affairs staff are unfamiliar with research on student learning in college and how student affairs staff influence that learning.

   Proposition: Student affairs staff are uncomfortable with the notion of fostering student learning because it implies an emphasis on the academic mission; we spend too much time worrying about being "second-class citizens" and too little time focusing on the core activities of our institutions.

   Proposition: The culture of student affairs work overemphasizes the importance of social and affective growth in college and underemphasizes cognitive and intellectual growth.

3. **In what ways do current student affairs assumptions, expectations, and practices foster student learning?**

   Proposition: Student affairs staff are the campus experts on students and their learning.

Proposition: Student affairs staff view the learner as a whole, and all aspects of the campus as learning environments.

Proposition: Many of the learning outcomes external constituents demand (e.g., teamwork, tolerance, empathy, communication, and leadership) can be effectively fostered in learning environments with which student affairs staff work most directly.

4. **How can successful partnerships be formed with our academic colleagues to achieve institutional goals for student learning?**

Proposition: Student affairs staff create obstacles to partnerships with faculty by reinforcing separations between in-class and out-of-class learning and neglecting explicit connections between in-class and out-of-class learning (e.g., asking students to reflect on how their work on student government implements what they have learned in political science, management, and sociology classes).

Proposition: Student affairs staff need to take initiative to form successful partnerships with academic colleagues.

Proposition: Student affairs staff are uncomfortable initiating partnerships with academic colleagues for a variety of reasons, including fear of appearing to want to be faculty, fear of not being taken seriously, and lack of experience communicating across the cultures of student affairs and academic affairs.

5. **How do we know our students are learning — and how do we know we influence that learning?**

Proposition: Student affairs staff offer out-of-class experiences to students as opportunities, as occasions at which something good will happen if students take advantage of them. But we do not know what, if anything, about these activities contributes to student learning.

Proposition: Student affairs staff must be more consciously purposeful — focused on student learning outcomes — and more clear and articulate about how student affairs work accomplishes those purposes. To accomplish that, student affairs staff must plan for student learning and assess student learning outcomes.

6. **What do student affairs staff need to know and be able to do to foster student learning?**

Proposition: Student affairs staff need to be familiar with theories of teaching and learning, and have experience using those theories in work with students.

Proposition: Student affairs staff just need to be good managers.

Proposition: Current curricula and experiences in student affairs preparation programs provide inadequate preparation for helping students learn.

MONOGRAPH OVERVIEW

These questions and propositions also are intended to serve as a framework for thinking about the research, ideas, and suggestions presented in the pages that follow. This monograph is presented in six chapters. In Chapter One, Rosalind Andreas and John Schuh scan challenges in the higher education landscape in the late 1990s and describe the imperative to focus on student learning as a means to address those challenges. George Kuh and Karen Arnold provide, in Chapter 2, a description of "mental models" of the purposes of undergraduate education as a means to illustrate the critical role assumptions and beliefs play in shifting to a learning-oriented view of student affairs work. In Chapter 3, Marcia Baxter Magolda defines, and redefines, student learning in the context of student affairs practice. Chapter 4 provides a brief review of research by Tom Miller and Elizabeth Whitt; college student learning, and how learning outcomes are influenced by out-of-class experiences and environments are described. In Chapter 5, Lee Upcraft and Ernest Pascarella offer a model for assessing and measuring learning outcomes. The monograph concludes with a description of steps that student affairs staff can take to implement our student learning imperative.

Colleagues whose ideas are reflected in the propositions document are the members of the Student Learning Project Work Group (Rosalind Andreas, Karen Arnold, Marcia Baxter Magolda, Jon Dalton, George Kuh, Tom Miller, Ernie Pascarella, Larry Roper, John Schuh, Pat Terenzini, and Lee Upcraft) and the 1996 NASPA Conference Planning Committee (Rosalind Andreas, David Bergen, Johnetta Cross Brazzell, Jill Carnaghi, Sheila Murphy, David Nestor, Larry Roper, and John Schuh).

Contributors

Rosalind E. Andreas is Associate Dean and Assistant Professor in the College of Education and Social Services at the University of Vermont (UVM). Prior to assuming these responsibilities, she was Vice President for Student Affairs at UVM, and Dean of Students at the University of Arizona and Oakland University. Rosalind received an M.A. in Speech Communication from the University of Kansas and her Ph.D. in higher education from University of Michigan. Active in NASPA, she has served as director of the Richard F. Stevens Institute, member of the editorial board of the *NASPA Journal*, and chair of the NASPA 1996 Conference Committee. Rosalind has written on leadership programs, commuter students, institutional planning, and student learning, and was a member of the research team for the College Experiences Study, which resulted in the Jossey-Bass publication *Involving Colleges*.

Karen Arnold is Associate Professor of Higher Education at Boston College. She received her Ph.D. in higher education at the University of Illinois, where she directed the Illinois Valedictorian Project. Her books on talent development and women in higher education include *Lives of Promise: What Becomes of High School Valedictorians, and Remarkable Women: Perspectives on Female Talent Development*. Karen has been very involved with the American Educational Research Association (AERA), the Association for the Study of Higher Education (ASHE), and ACPA. She is an associate editor of the *Review of Higher Education* and serves on the board of the *Educational Researcher*.

Marcia Baxter Magolda is Professor of Educational Leadership at Miami University. She received her masters and Ph.D. from The Ohio State University in College Student

Personnel/Higher Education. Her scholarship addresses the evolution of epistemological development in college and young adult life, and her books include *Knowing and Reasoning in College* (Jossey-Bass, 1992). Marcia is active in AERA, ASHE, and ACPA. She serves on the Board of Contributors of *About Campus* and is an ACPA Senior Scholar. She was recently named as one of forty young leaders in academe by *Change* magazine.

George D. Kuh is Professor of Higher Education and Associate Dean of the Faculties at Indiana University Bloomington where he directs the College Student Experiences Questionnaire Research and Distribution Program. He received his master's degree from St. Cloud State University (MN) and his Ph.D. from University of Iowa. George's recent research and writing address such topics as undergraduate education, assessments of student engagement and learning, campus environments, the institutional conditions that foster student learning, and collaboration between academic and student affairs. An ACPA Senior Scholar Diplomate, George has received awards from ACPA and NASPA for his extensive contributions to research and scholarship in higher education and student affairs. He is immediate-past-president of ASHE, a member of the Board of Contributors of *About Campus*, and was co-principal investigator of the College Experiences Study and co-author of *Involving Colleges*.

Thomas E. Miller is Vice President for Student Affairs and Dean of Students at Eckerd College in St. Petersburg, Florida. A graduate of Muhlenberg College, he continued his studies at Indiana University where he was awarded M.S. and Ed.D. degrees in higher education and student affairs administration. Tom has served NASPA as regional vice president (Region II) from 1982-85, at-large representative to the national Board of Directors, member of national conference committees in 1992 and 1995, and member of the editorial board of the *NASPA Journal*. He also chaired development of NASPA's *Reasonable Expectations* document and served as NASPA's interassociational delegate to the task force working on the Joint Statement of Rights and Freedoms of Students.

Ernest T. Pascarella is the Mary Louise Petersen Professor of Higher Education at the University of Iowa. He received his B.A. from Princeton University, his M.A. from the University of Pennsylvania and his Ph.D. from Syracuse University. Prior to coming to UI, he was a professor at the University of Illinois at Chicago. Ernie has focused his research and writing on the impact of college on students and student persistence. Among his more than 130 publications is *How College Affects Students* (1991), written with Patrick T. Terenzini. Ernie's contributions to scholarship in higher education have been recognized with awards from the Association for Institutional Research (AIR), ASHE, AERA, ACPA, NASPA, and the University of Illinois, and he is an ACPA Senior Scholar Diplomate.

John H. Schuh is Professor and Chair of Educational Leadership and Policy Studies at Iowa State University. Previously he held administrative and faculty appointments at Arizona State University, Indiana University (Bloomington) and Wichita Sate University. John received his graduate degrees in counseling and higher education from Arizona State University. He has been recognized for research and publication by NASPA and ACPA, including ACPA Senior Scholar, and for leadership and service by ACUHO-I. John received a Fulbright award to study higher education in Germany in 1994. Currently he is editor in chief of the *New Directions for the Student Services* sourcebooks and associate editor of the *Journal of College Student Development*. John was co-principal investigator of the College Experiences Study and co-author of *Involving Colleges*.

M. Lee Upcraft is a Research Associate in the Center for the Study of Higher Education, Affiliate Professor Emeritus of Higher Education, and Assistant Vice President Emeritus for Student Affairs at Penn State University. He received his BA in social studies and MA in Guidance and Counseling from SUNY Albany, and his Ph.D in Student Personnel Administration from Michigan State University. He is an ACPA Senior Scholar Diplomate and received the Outstanding Contribution to Research or Literature from NASPA. Lee has published extensively on such topics as student retention, residence halls, drugs and alcohol, student affairs administration, and assessment in student affairs.

Elizabeth J. Whitt is Associate Professor and Coordinator of the Student Development in Postsecondary Education program at the University of Iowa. She received graduate degrees in college student personnel from Michigan State University and higher education administration and sociology from Indiana University. Prior to moving to the University of Iowa, Liz was a faculty member at Iowa State University and

University of Illinois at Chicago, and a student affairs administrator at University of Nebraska-Lincoln and Doane College. A past member of the Board of Directors of NASPA, she now serves on the editorial board of the *Journal of College Student Development* and is associate editor of the *New Directions for Student Services* sourcebooks. Liz also was co-author of *Involving Colleges* and served as co-chair of the ACPA-NASPA task force on *Principles of Good Practice for Student Affairs.*

Acknowledgments

This book is the result of the collaboration not only of the contributors whose names are listed here, but of countless student affairs professionals who participated in discussions about implementation and implications of the *Student Learning Imperative* (ACPA, 1994) at the 1996 NASPA Conference in Atlanta and at other forums on student learning and student affairs between 1996 and 1998. Special recognition and thanks are due Charles Schroeder (University of Missouri), former president of ACPA, and the other authors of the *SLI*, for challenging us to "redefine the role of student affairs to intentionally promote student learning," and to Jon Dalton (Florida State University), former president of NASPA, for bringing this important conversation to NASPA. Our profession owes all of them a debt of gratitude.

Despite the excellent efforts of the chapter authors and other contributors, however, the monograph could not have been published without the efforts of Margaret Healy (Mankato State University). This was the last of the monographs commissioned during Margi's tenure as editor of the NASPA Monograph series and her suggestions, support, and persistence made it possible for me to finish what all of us had started. I thank her, publicly, for her help and her friendship. Finally, the book benefited from the comments of reviewers from the Monograph Board and Patrick Love (Kent State University), Monograph Series Editor.

Elizabeth J. Whitt
Iowa City, Iowa
August 1998

CHAPTER 1

The Student Affairs Landscape: Focus On Learning

Rosalind E. Andreas • *John H. Schuh*

> *We can't advance as long as we're holding tight to what no longer works.*
> *And we have to break the mold before a new form can emerge.*
> — Guskin, 1997, p. 9

Few would characterize the 1990s as a "Golden Age" for postsecondary education. Problems inside and outside the nearly 3700 colleges and universities make this a difficult time for faculty, administrators and students. In fact, at the time of his retirement from the American Council on Education in 1994, Robert Atwell asserted that during the more than forty years of his involvement with higher education, "...we have never faced as many difficult challenges as we do today" (1994, p.125).

The purpose of this chapter is twofold. First, we examine the key challenges on the higher education and student affairs landscape; what obstacles do we face to doing our work effectively and surviving and thriving in this time of rapid change? Second, we describe and discuss methods to meet those challenges and overcome our obstacles. As noted in the Preface, at a critical time in the American civil rights movement thirty years ago, Dr. Martin Luther King, Jr. called his colleagues to "sober reflection" about the obstacles they faced and assess the effectiveness of their current methods. In this time of challenge and change in higher education, King's advice provides direction for us as well.

"SOBER REFLECTION" ON OBSTACLES

The "obstacles," or challenges, that dot the landscape of American higher education at the close of the twentieth century include unprecedented change, scarce (and shrinking) financial resources, and a growing lack of public confidence in higher education's ability — even willingness — to achieve its missions and goals effectively and efficiently. Each of these challenges does, of course, influence — and so enhance the impact of — the others.

Challenge: Unprecedented Change
Students

Students who come to our institutions are more diverse than ever on all dimensions, including age, race, ethnicity, language, ability, and experience (Astin, 1998; Levine & Cureton, 1998a, 1998b). This diversity has added richness to our campuses and brought challenges to old ways of thinking about curricula, as well as instructional and service delivery. Colleges and universities also face the challenges involved in attracting and retaining more students of color, as well as students from other traditionally underrepresented groups, so that campuses more closely resemble the society their graduates will serve and lead (London, 1996; Rendon, 1996, 1998).

An increasingly diverse student body challenges colleges to provide all students with the assistance and opportunities they need to achieve their educational goals. Today's students bring to campus a broad range of personal, economic, cultural, social, community, and political issues that must be addressed if they are to learn effectively (Astin, 1998; London, 1996; Newton, 1998; Rendon, 1996, 1998; Levine & Cureton, 1998a, 1998b). Some observers of higher education fear, however, that our current methods of undergraduate education are "better organized to discourage students —to weed them out — than [they are] to cultivate and support our most important national resource, our people" (Wingspread Group, 1993, p. 5).

Electronic Technologies

Technological advances have precipitated fundamental shifts in how courses are delivered and how students learn (Schwitzer, 1997). Electronic technologies make it possible, for example, for students to register, obtain advising, receive career counseling, look for work, and have conversations with peers and faculty without leaving their rooms. Such technologies also allow students to take courses by television or satellite, and never sit in the same room with their instructors or fellow students, thereby expanding access to our institutions far beyond the boundaries of our campuses. The costs and complexity of creating and maintaining up-to-date electronic educational technologies are daunting, especially in a time of contracting funds, and especially for small, private colleges. Yet the public believes that higher education has been much too slow to use new technologies to revolutionize its work, restructure its organizations, and prepare students for current and future realities (Pew, 1994).

Other challenges — besides funding — posed by expanding electronic technologies include meeting the needs of a very diverse and widely dispersed student body while creating a sense of involvement and community (Schwitzer, 1997). In addition, what are the implications of the expanding use of electronic networks and services for student affairs professionals? What, for example, are the implications for residence halls, student activities, or career development centers of widespread use of the Internet to teach college courses to persons in their homes and places of employment?

Restructuring and Reengineering

A typical combination of responses to rapid change on campuses across the country has been reorganization, restructuring, and reengineering in an effort to increase efficiency and effectiveness and improve delivery of instruction and educational services. Reducing costs while improving student learning require, some argue, dramatically decreasing the size of — and duplication of services from — many administrative units, including student services (Ballou, 1997; Guskin, 1994a, 1994b). For example, in his 1994 *Change* article on improving administrative productivity in higher education, Antioch University Chancellor Alan Guskin made the following assertion:

> Strategically, enhancing student learning and reducing student costs are, in my judgment the primary yardstick [for organizational effectiveness]. *Since the faculty and academic areas are most directly tied to student learning, alterations in the lower priority support areas must precede* [major changes in the role of the faculty] [emphasis added] (1994a, p. 29).

Widespread fear that such sentiments foreshadow the demise of student affairs organizations as we know them, such as by folding student affairs functions into the work of academic services, increasingly is reflected in electronic mail discussions and professional association programs.

CHALLENGE: SCARCE RESOURCES

Underlying these unprecedented changes is the challenge of shrinking financial resources, and increased competition for those resources that *are* available. Some experts have stated that the primary financial challenge faced by higher education is not "to increase the revenue stream, but to reduce expenditures" (Atwell, 1994, p. 29). Although most persons involved in higher education today are familiar with — and probably accept — the call to "do more with less," Arthur Levine, President of Columbia Teacher's College and a well-known higher education scholar, has contradicted that notion with what is perhaps a more realistic assessment: "The common wisdom is that higher education must do more with less today. The reality is that institutions will have to do *less* with less" (1997, p. 32).

Changes in federal fiscal policies and priorities have had a dramatic effect on the capacity of states to meet the needs of their constituents, including needs for education (Schuh, 1993). While substantial funds remain committed to research, the federal budget's contribution to funding higher education is declining (Atwell, 1994). In practical terms this means that state budgets are stretched to provide basic services and to protect citizens, and public higher education is only one of many state entities seeking a share of the financial pie. It is likely that the struggle over resources will only intensify as competition for public resources increases and the workforce to fund public support decreases (Kerr, 1994).

Declining governmental support for higher education, including requiring public universities to compete with other state agencies for funds, is unprecedented in recent higher education history. Until recently, expanding access to public postsecondary education was an important priority for many state legislatures, as well as the federal government, a priority that was reflected in unquestioned allocations of public funds (Levine, 1997). In the 1990s, however,

> American higher education has become a mature industry. More than
> 60 percent of all high school graduates is now going on to

postsecondary education. This matriculation rate is being viewed in state capitols as sufficient or even as an over-expansion of higher education (Levine, 1997, p. 31).

As a result of shrinking public sources of funding for higher education, faculty and administrators at both public and private colleges must spend more time engaged in entrepreneurial behavior to generate revenue and less time with students to promote their learning and personal development (Schuh, 1993).

The shift in sources of public funding also have an impact on the key constituency of postsecondary education: students. In his review of the challenges facing colleges and universities in the 1990s, Robert Atwell noted, "of all the forces I have mentioned, the most disturbing is the effort to shift the burden of college from society and family toward the student" (Atwell, 1994, p. 129). In 1995, the push to balance the federal budget caused legislators to propose reductions in loan interest subsidies, self-help aid, and grants, a move which reduced support to both students and institutions.

Loans have become the most common form of financial aid. The average amount of student debt accumulated during the four or five years of an undergraduate education rose from $2,500 in 1988-89 (Topper, 1994) to $7,675 in 1990 and $8,473 in 1993 (Goodman, 1995). This debt burden can limit access to college and likely will contribute to society's inability to support an educated populace.

Another response to the withdrawal of federal, state, and other sources of support has been an increase in tuition at most institutions. This has contributed to the "sticker shock" which has overwhelmed and angered the public and invited unwelcome, but not surprising, involvement of policy makers (Wingspread Report, 1993). Recall the 1997 *Time* magazine cover story on the cost of going to college, titled "Gouging U." The message is clear: higher education costs too much for what it is perceived to provide.

CHALLENGE: A CRISIS OF CONFIDENCE

Signs of waning confidence in higher education's ability to make a difference in the lives of students and society are everywhere. And this waning confidence is accompanied by increasing demands, and higher standards, for accountability (Guskin, 1997). This can be attributed, at least in part, to the shift to the status of a mature industry. Levine (1997) noted that "Government treats mature industries very different from growth industries . . . It asks hard questions about their cost, efficiency, productivity, and effectiveness . . . It reduces their autonomy, increases their regulation, and demands greater accountability" (p. 31).

The Wingspread Group (1993) summarized this crisis of confidence in the strongest terms — terms colleges and universities ignore at their peril:

> A disturbing and dangerous mismatch exists between what American society needs of higher education and what it is receiving. Nowhere is the mismatch more dangerous than in the quality of undergraduate preparation . . . What does our society NEED from higher education? It needs stronger, more vital forms of community. It needs an informed and involved citizenry. It needs graduates able to assume leadership roles in American life . . . Above all, it needs a commitment to the idea that all Americans have an opportunity to develop their talents to the fullest. *Higher education is not meeting these imperatives* (p. 1-4).

A NEW DAWN: THE LEARNING PARADIGM

The consensus among all the recent higher education reform efforts (e.g., Boyer Commission, 1998; NASULGC, 1997; Wingspread, 1993) is that we can, and should, meet our imperatives — that is, educating more people and educating them much more effectively to know how to learn, and to be self-directed and flexible — by "putting student learning first [and] focusing overwhelmingly on what our students learn and what they achieve" (Wingspread Group, 1993, p. 13).

The fact that this emphasis on learning has been described as a "paradigm shift" for higher education might seem surprising. Have colleges and universities not always "put student learning first"? Many have argued — persuasively —, however, that higher education has put instruction — not learning — first (Barr & Tagg, 1995). Within the old paradigm, the purpose of college was to provide instruction; the new paradigm views colleges as institutions which exist to produce learning.

> The Learning Paradigm envisions the institution itself as a learner . . .
>
> In the Learning Paradigm, a college's purpose is not to transfer knowledge, but to create environments and experiences that bring students to discover and conduct knowledge for themselves, to make

students members of communities of learners that make discoveries and solve problems. The college aims, in fact, to create a series of ever more powerful learning environments (Barr & Tagg, 1995, p. 14, 15).

And, Barr and Tagg asserted, "this shift changes everything" (p. 13).

The National Association of State Universities and Land Grant Colleges (NASULGC) picked up on, and moved forward with, this theme in their 1997 report, *Returning to our Roots: The Student Experience*. The authors of that report expanded on the notion of learning as the primary focus of higher education:

As we understand the term, learning is not something reserved for classrooms or degree programs. It is available to every member of the academic community, whether in the classroom or the administration building, the laboratory or the library, the residence halls or the performing arts center . . . Learning is available to all and all serve learning (p. 17).

This shift does, indeed, change everything, including student affairs work. As long as colleges existed to provide instruction, only persons engaged in instruction — traditionally defined — worked at the core of the institution. Recall the quotation from Guskin (1994a) earlier in this chapter. When colleges exist to provide learning, however, everyone who works with students has the responsibility and the obligation to foster learning, and so to be involved in the core purpose of the enterprise. If a college's purpose is to create "ever more powerful learning environments" and learning is not reserved to the classroom, student affairs practice can take on a central role. And so, although this shift from a focus on instruction to a focus on learning changes everything, it does so in ways that bode very well for the role of student affairs professionals in colleges and universities. That is, as long as student affairs professionals respond effectively to the shift.

THE STUDENT LEARNING IMPERATIVE

The Preface to this monograph described one response of the student affairs profession to the shift to a learning paradigm: *The Student Learning Imperative (SLI)* (ACPA, 1994) and subsequent efforts to identify and describe ways in which student affairs can meet *our* learning imperative effectively. The *SLI* described student affairs work in terms of fostering student learning, and working with other members of the campus community — including faculty and students — to create powerful learning environments.

> Thus, student affairs programs and services must be designed and managed with specific student learning and personal development outcomes in mind . . . [Furthermore], if learning is the primary measure of institutional productivity by which the quality of undergraduate education is determined, what and how much students learn also must be the criteria by which the value of student affairs is judged (as contrasted with numbers of programs offered or clients served) (ACPA, 1994, p. 2).

Using student learning as a criterion for measuring the effectiveness of student affairs work? This really *does* change everything!

The *SLI* argued that, to participate effectively in "putting student learning first," student affairs professionals must create learning-oriented student affairs organizations. These are places where:

1.   the student affairs mission complements and reinforces the institution's mission of learning. In addition, achieving student learning — in the form of desired educational outcomes — is the primary goal for student affairs policies, services, and programs;
2.   resources are allocated to foster student learning;
3.   student affairs staff collaborate with colleagues in other areas of the institution to plan for, and foster, student learning;
4.   student affairs staff are experts on students, their environments, and teaching and learning processes; and
5.   policies and practices are grounded in research and institutional assessment on student learning outcomes.

In general, these are seamless learning environments which do not divide students' experiences with labels such as "academic" and "non-academic" or "in-class" and "out-of-class" (Kuh, 1996; Kuh, Branch Douglas, Lund, & Raymin-Gyurnik, 1994; Kuh, Schuh, Whitt, & Associates, 1991). Rather, students are assisted to "use their life experiences to make meaning of material introduced in classes, laboratories, and studios, and to apply what they are learning in class to their lives outside the classroom" (Kuh, 1996, p. 136).

SUMMARY

Higher education faces a landscape "dotted" with obstacles — challenges of crises of confidence, unprecedented change, competition over resources, and escalating costs for students and families. Charting a course, and leading a march, across this new and uncertain terrain toward our imperatives is, perhaps, the greatest challenge of all. Yet "it is imperative that we do better. There really is no alternative" (Levine, 1997, p. 32). In the following chapter, Karen Arnold and George Kuh describe the importance of how we — and others within our institutions — view what matters in undergraduate education for meeting our imperatives effectively.

CHAPTER 2

What Matters in Undergraduate Education? Mental Models, Student Learning, and Student Affairs

Karen Arnold • George D. Kuh

Posted on the Internet recently was the Ivy League version of the joke: "How many [people] are needed to screw in a light bulb?" The answer ascribed to Harvard was: "Only one, to hold the bulb—the world revolves around Cambridge."

Popular among New Yorkers is their "Map of the World." In this poster, Manhattan skyscrapers dominate the foreground. Some distance from the center and much smaller in scale are Brooklyn and the Statue of Liberty. Washington, D.C. is but a small circle; London and Paris are merely dots. The remainder of the globe is relegated to an area the size of Central Park. The meaning is clear: New York City is the center of the universe. The rest of the world exists only in relation to Manhattan. The New York poster is not an actual landscape, of course, but a mental model of how some people view the world and their place in it. Other major cities have their own versions, all with skewed perspectives in which local vistas dominate.

Although colleges and universities do not advertise such posters (at least none that we know of), it is appropriate to ask questions about how faculty, student affairs staff, and students at any given institution view their world and their places in it. How are others – and others' priorities - depicted in their "maps" of the collegiate landscape? Answering such questions can elicit interesting, and sometimes disturbing, constructions of what various groups think really matters in colleges and universities.

In this chapter we examine assumptions about undergraduate learning and personal development that guide faculty, student affairs professionals, and students. These assumptions and beliefs are the basis for "mental models" of the world, a sort of navigational system that guides thought and behavior in an almost unconscious manner (Senge, 1990). By examining what each group considers to be central to desired outcomes of undergraduate education we attempt to make explicit some tacit assumptions and beliefs that shape what each group values and how they behave. The process of identifying mental models also can help channel institutional efforts toward what really matters in undergraduate education.

We begin by summarizing what prompted this examination of the influence of mental models on undergraduate education. Then we describe and analyze the mental models of faculty, student affairs professionals, and students, including some first-order implications. We conclude with a brief discussion of the consequences of the various models for fostering a common view of learning and what student affairs professionals might do in response.

DISCOVERING WHAT MATTERS IN UNDERGRADUATE EDUCATION

During initial discussions of the NASPA-sponsored Student Learning Project Work Group we realized that only after understanding what faculty, student affairs staff, and students consider to be central to student learning, and comparing those views with the research on college student development, could a common vision of student learning be created. Understanding differing versions of "what matters" in undergraduate education was necessary to develop the shared language and complementary practices necessary to establish seamless learning environments.

One way to discover what people believe about undergraduate education is to ask such questions as: "What does our institution value?" "What are we trying to accomplish?" "How do various groups spend their time?" "How do I spend my time?" "What can I do to have a greater impact on my students?" Frequently embedded in the responses of faculty, student affairs professionals, and academic administrators to these and similar questions are assumptions, beliefs, and expectations—for themselves, their colleagues, and their students.

The Student Learning Project Work Group developed a set of abstract figures to approximate the views of faculty, student affairs administrators, and students about what matters to student learning and personal development. Although the six models presented in this chapter are not derived from empirical research, we believe they are generally consistent with the theory and research about student learning and life in institutions of higher education and our experience in working with faculty, student affairs staff, and students in different types of institutions.

These models were critiqued and modified through dialogue with student affairs graduate students, professionals and faculty members at association meetings (ACPA, ASHE, AERA, NASPA) and institution-based colloquia (e.g., Earlham College, Monroe Community College, Ithaca College, Portland State University, University of Western Ontario, University of Vermont, Wake Forest University). An earlier version of the first three models appeared in Kuh, Branch Douglas, Lund, and Ramin-Gyurnek (1994).

The figures depict the mental models of faculty, student affairs professionals, and students. In the center or core of the models are activities and experiences that each group believes are absolutely vital to student learning and personal development. The concentric circles emanating from the core represent activities, functions, and experiences that are more or less important. The closer to the center, the more integral the function, activity, or experience. The further from the center, the less important the elements to student learning and personal development from the point of view of the particular group.

The figures are heuristic devices, intended to stimulate discussion and research about the ways in which competing visions of undergraduate education may facilitate or hinder the attainment of a seamless learning environment for undergraduates. Everything about the models is open to discussion and debate. For example, such areas as service learning, internships, and orientation might change the position in the faculty mental model depending on how well connected these activities are to the academic program. In some institutions the term "research," which is used in the faculty mental model to represent scholarly inquiry, suggests intellectual activity which is too narrowly circumscribed to embrace much of what the faculty do in the way of discipline-based inquiry; such institutions might prefer the term "scholarship."

The value of the figures presented here lies in the questions they raise and the analyses they provoke. The models can be modified to reflect more accurately a particular institution's context. Some institutions may find that the models have limited utility. This is entirely acceptable, *provided* that in the process of coming to this conclusion faculty, student affairs staff, and students reach a better understanding of "what matters" to student learning and personal development and discover additional ways that they can collaborate to attain valued outcomes of undergraduate education.

WHAT MATTERS TO FACULTY

Figure 1 displays what professors believe is important to undergraduate learning. In this model, the curriculum, teaching, and scholarship constitute the core. The central activities include transmitting the content and methods of an academic discipline, facilitating intellectual development in a domain of thought, and producing knowledge to advance a field. The key settings where such activities regularly occur are classrooms, laboratories, and studios.

Just beyond the core are functions and activities that directly or indirectly support acquisition of knowledge and skills students need to master academic tasks. Registration, admissions, financial aid, and academic advising functions are needed to assign adequately-prepared students to the appropriate courses and programs of study and to perform general administrative functions (e.g., organizing and managing faculty and staff activities, coordinating the curriculum). This ring also includes additional instructional settings: the library, learning center, computer clusters, study abroad, cooperative education, and internships.

Further from the center are non-academic services that assist many students in taking advantage of the institution's resources for learning: residence halls assumed to be conducive to study (though this is not always the case), child care services that permit student-parents to attend classes, activities and events that foster congenial relations between faculty and students, and orientation programs and career services which assist students in transition. Faculty view these activities as legitimate, but not central to attaining core tasks.

The outermost ring contains services and activities that preoccupy students when they are neither in a formal instructional setting nor preparing for classes. These

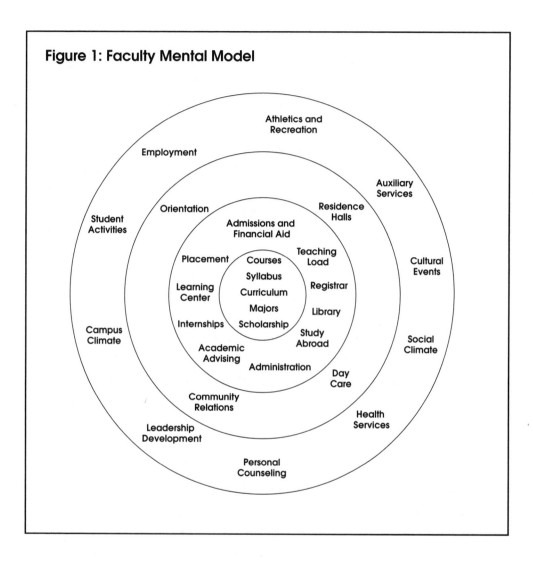

Figure 1: Faculty Mental Model

include the myriad social and recreational activities that undergraduates organize on their own, on and off campus, and the formal co-curriculum (e.g., institutionally-sponsored student organizations, leadership development, judicial affairs, recreation, cultural activities, and entertainment events). From the faculty's point of view, these activities are not necessary to attain the institution's educational mission. Some of these are mild distractions; others are contradictory to educational purposes (e.g., events that encourage binge drinking or which ridicule women and people of color). Student welfare services (e.g., personal counseling, health services) are considered unnecessary as they are not fundamentally educational in structure or purpose.

Implications

Many plausible versions of faculty mindscapes of undergraduate learning surely exist (e.g., individual, disciplinary, institutional). Generally speaking, however, we are confident that the majority of faculty would agree that the academic program and classroom activities are the most important aspects of a college and contribute to undergraduate learning far more than any of the other activities and elements that appear (or do not appear) on their "mental map." Assuming this is the case, the curriculum and academic activities (teaching, studying) are the most important components of undergraduate learning as far as faculty are concerned. They do not consider personal and social development to be central, a view that conflicts with statements of college goals in most institutional catalogues.

In addition, faculty assume little or no responsibility for students and their learning beyond the classroom. Whatever undergraduates do or learn beyond formal academic settings is unrelated to the primary learning goals of the academy. The further from the core, the more limited the contact with faculty. This view is unfortunate as research shows the almost uniform positive impact of faculty-student interaction outside the classroom (Astin, 1993; Kuh, 1993; Pascarella & Terenzini, 1991). Faculty also assume that students should organize their lives around formal academic study, focusing their time and energy to academic content mastery and intellectual skills. The academic program takes up (or should consume) most of students' time. Vocational preparation is a function of students selecting an intrinsically interesting college major, mastering this discipline, and acquiring the requisite cognitive skills.

Activities in the outer ring such as employment or leadership experiences in student organizations are distractions from that which contributes directly to "real" or highly valued forms of learning. In fact, many faculty see certain of these activities competing for student attention and effort, detracting from the academic work that really matters.

WHAT MATTERS TO STUDENT AFFAIRS PROFESSIONALS

Figure 2 depicts what student affairs professionals think is important to student learning and personal development. As with the faculty model, academic courses are in the core. In sharp contrast to the faculty model, however, the student affairs cognitive map includes in the center the formal co-curriculum and campus life, at least for traditional-age students who live on campus. What matters most to student affairs professionals is promoting student involvement in activities that are assumed to foster student development. Three intentionally-designed learning sites—classrooms, student organizations and other co-curricular activities, and residence halls—are represented in the core. Such activities as participating in student government, writing for the school paper, joining a special-interest club, and living in a residence hall are considered vital to learning and development. By becoming active in the campus community, students benefit from the synergistic interplay

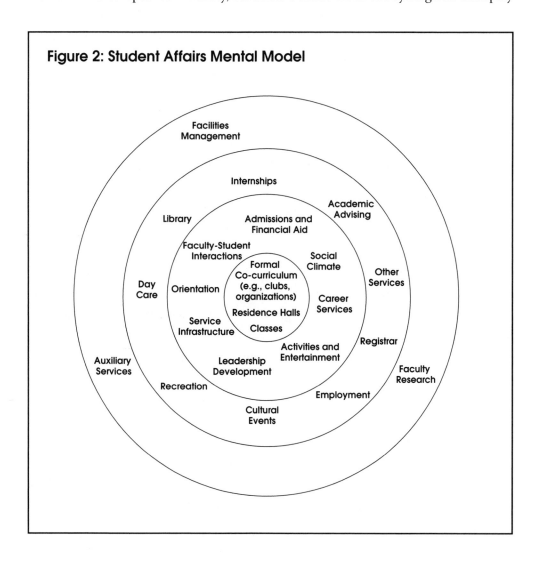

Figure 2: Student Affairs Mental Model

among curricular, co-curricular, and residential experiences. Indeed, the experience of living with others is a sort of "learning laboratory" in which students increase both their self-knowledge and their ability to live and work within communities of diverse individuals.

The ring just beyond the core contains areas student affairs professionals consider important if students are to take advantage of opportunities inherent in various institutional learning environments. At most institutions, these activities and services are performed by student affairs personnel. As with the faculty model, admissions and financial aid and general administration are in this ring. The rationale for these functions differs somewhat from the faculty mindscape, however. Student affairs professionals believe these programs and services ensure an optimal match between the individual student and the institution and help students take advantage of resources for learning and personal development. The service infrastructure (e.g., personal counseling, off-campus housing assistance, student unions, dining halls) includes resources some students need to attain their learning goals. Orientation events are important because they engage students in both social and academic activities. Career services, leadership development, and community involvement are venues that connect academic programs with students' lives beyond the classroom. They are also settings where students acquire interpersonal and practical competence, skills not directly addressed in many classes and majors but which are necessary for success after college in the arenas of family and work (Kuh, 1993, 1995). Finally, this ring also includes the social climate created through peer and faculty interactions as well as events, programs, and entertainment on campus, that are positively related to satisfaction and some dimensions of personal development (Pace, 1990; Pascarella & Terenzini, 1991).

The second ring out from the core contains student activities and services that are often popular among students (and in which substantial institutional and student resources are invested). However, these activities are not considered intentionally designed learning environments. Using recreational facilities and participating in social events, for instance, are neither required by most academic programs, nor do students or student affairs professionals describe them as learning opportunities. (Should this be doubted, simply ask whether student affairs has data that link participation in these activities with desired outcomes of college.) Such services as day care, registration, and the library are services that enable students to participate fully in the academic and social life of the campus core. Similarly, employment allows students to meet the expenses of college. As with the faculty model, however, employment is not thought to be directly related to student learning. In fact, both employment and off-campus internships take time and effort away from involvement in campus life. However, this view is not supported by the college outcomes research which shows a positive link between such activities and certain valued outcomes (e.g., practical competence) (Kuh, 1995; Pascarella, Edison, Nora, Hagedorn, & Terenzini, 1998; Pascarella & Terenzini, 1991).

The outer ring of the student affairs mental model contains the management of academic facilities and personnel, business affairs, and other so-called auxiliary services. It also includes faculty research, an activity that many student affairs professionals do not fully appreciate and which many consider to compete with more important activities, such as teaching, advising, and informal interactions with students outside the classroom (except for students with whom they may be collaborating on research).

It is also interesting to note that scholarship does not appear in any part of the student affairs "map." This lack of attention to scholarship could inhibit student affairs professionals from incorporating research-based thinking into their practice. Furthermore, it could be perceived by faculty and other academic colleagues as disregard, disrespect, or disinterest for an important mission of higher education: creation and dissemination of new knowledge.

Implications

The student affairs mental model differs from that of the faculty by not featuring the curriculum, teaching, or scholarship in the core. Rather, the model presumes that personal development is an acceptable, even a central, value of the academy (Chickering, 1981). Courses, curricula, and majors are differentiated from meaningful, personalized learning about self and one's place in the world. Academic programs are important but not equivalent to a broader view of undergraduate education that encompasses intrapersonal and interpersonal learning.

As with the faculty model, the student affairs view distinguishes between in-class and out-of-class experiences but reverses the order of their importance to desired outcomes of college. And unlike the faculty, student affairs professionals believe that the most powerful lessons in college come from contacts with peers and from making meaning of personal experiences. The model implies that meaningful learning occurs primarily in certain formal, intentional out-of-classroom experiences. This implies that students benefit if they participate fully in institution-sponsored activities and organizations, live in campus residences, and have meaningful contact with faculty outside the classroom and with residence life staff and programs. On the other hand, student employment (particularly off campus) interferes with what really matters in undergraduate education by limiting the amount of time working students can spend on campus participating in institutional events and activities.

By performing essentially non-academic activities student affairs detaches itself from the curriculum, faculty research, and the intellectual life of the institution. This view absolves student affairs professionals from understanding what faculty do or from helping students integrate what they are learning inside the classroom with their lives outside the classroom. Thus, faculty and undergraduates accurately perceive student affairs to be unconnected in purpose and function to the institution's academic mission.

WHAT MATTERS TO STUDENTS

Undergraduate students are so diverse that no single model, even those as general as the faculty and student affairs models presented above, can adequately account for the views of American college students about what they think is important to their education. For this reason, three models were developed to approximate mindscapes of what students think matters to their learning. The first (Figure 3) represents the view of 18-24 year old undergraduates enrolled full time and who live on campus. The second model is for traditional-age full- and part-time commuter students (Figure 4). Finally, Figure 5 depicts the learning mindscape of the "new majority" (Astin, 1998; Ehrlich, 1991; Levine & Cureton, 1998a, 1998b), students age 25 or older (who comprise more than 40% of undergraduates).

Traditional-age Students in Residence

The lives of traditional-age residential students focus on the people and activities of their campus (Figure 3). Friendships and academic success are at the center. Consistent with psycho-social theory (Chickering & Reisser, 1993; Loevinger, 1976), being accepted by one's peers is the overwhelming preoccupation for the majority of

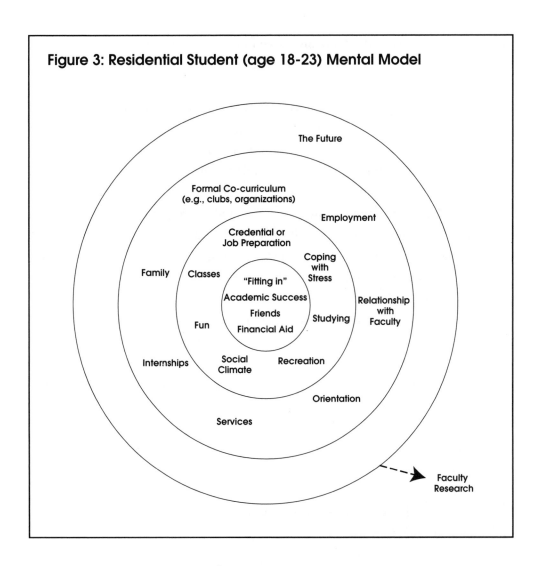

Figure 3: Residential Student (age 18-23) Mental Model

students. Students tend to focus on the instrumental aspects of the curriculum, defining academic success in terms of good grades, progress towards the degree, and job credentials (Horowitz, 1987).

In the ring just outside the core are activities that contribute to social integration (e.g., hanging out with friends, dating, attending social gatherings, and enjoying recreation and entertainment), which is positively related to persistence (Pascarella & Terenzini, 1991; Tinto, 1993), and activities that represent an instrumental view of academic performance (e.g., career selection, class attendance, preparation for course assignments). Also important is coping with the stress induced by the need to juggle pressures to perform academically, to fit in socially, to manage one's time and finances, and to make future-oriented decisions.

The next ring includes activities and services that attract the attention of relatively few students. Interactions with faculty, for example, are distant from the center of the college experience for most traditional undergraduates, particularly first-year students, many of whom are disinterested or intimidated by talking one-on-one with a faculty member (Baxter Magolda, 1992). Employment and the formal co-curriculum of school-sponsored activities and organizations are at the core of undergraduate life for only a minority of students (Moffatt, 1989). Other programs and services listed here become salient only to the small fraction of students who seek assistance. A socially isolated student, for example, might use the institution's counseling services, or a student undecided about the major field might seek out an academic advisor or attend a workshop offered by career services.

The map of many residential students allocates little space to the world beyond the campus. Whether parents and family are important depends on the individual student; ethnicity and family experience with higher education often are mediating factors. That is, for example, the support of, and regular contact with, parents and siblings are essential for many Mexican American students (Attinasi, 1989; Rendon, 1996, 1998) and many students who are first in their family to attend college (London, 1997; Rendon, 1996; Rose, 1989). In addition to the off-campus world, the outer ring for students also acknowledges auxiliary services such as buildings and grounds and the (dimly) imagined future. Finally, faculty research and the cultural and intellectual life of the campus are so far from the center of the lives of most undergraduates that they are "off the map."

Traditional-Age Commuter Students

When compared with their counterparts who live on campus, traditional-age commuter students have a somewhat different view of what matters to their learning (Figure 4). Many of these students commute from their parents' home to a nearby college or university. As with residential students, acceptance by peers is important to commuter students. They, too, define academic success in terms of grades, requirements, and degrees, and concentrate on the instrumental purposes of college—obtaining vocational credentials and occupational skills. For this group of students, however, friendships outside the institution (e.g., friends from high school) are often of central importance. Also in the core are concerns that do not appear in the residential students' mental model: logistical and psychological challenges associated with school, home and employment (which for many is full-time). These include arranging transportation to and from the institution, scheduling classes around transportation availability and work schedules, and juggling home and work responsibilities with their studies (Jacoby, 1989).

The ring just beyond the core acknowledges concerns about accessibility of parking, academic facilities, and study space, and the stress associated with managing logistical details and daily transitions between home, place of

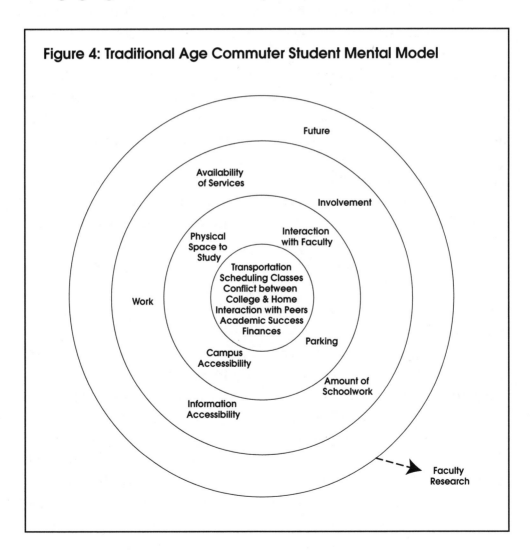

Figure 4: Traditional Age Commuter Student Mental Model

employment, and school. Faculty interactions also appear here, indicating that they are one of the most important connections between commuter students and their institution. Indeed, for many commuting students, the classroom and their instructors are their only connections.

As with their traditional age counterparts living in campus residences, the institutional resources in the next ring become salient only when students need to use them. Also included here are activities that consume a good deal of the commuter student's time and effort: paid employment, academic work, and opportunities for social engagement, either on campus or in the larger community. The formal co-curriculum, residence life, and auxiliary services are tangential. Finally, as with their age peers in residence, commuters pay little attention to faculty scholarship.

Undergraduates Over Age 25

The vocational aspirations of new majority students are often clearly focused. Many sacrifice considerable income and family time to attend college. More than any other group, they want assurances that their degree is marketable in the labor force. They also bring considerable life experience to the classroom (e.g., in child-rearing, as full-time workers). Because they balance family, employment, and school, their involvement in campus life is largely restricted to class attendance, faculty conferences, and programs and services that support their studies (Kuh, Vesper, & Krehbiel, 1994; Schlossberg, Lynch, & Chickering, 1989). Many of their concerns and ideas about what matters to learning overlap with those of younger commuting students. As was the case with traditional-age commuters, finances and logistical issues (e.g., transportation, parking, course scheduling, service availability) loom large for the older students.

The first ring out from the core includes functions and activities that personalize students' education by taking into account their background, previous experiences, and current circumstances. Teaching needs, personal attention, and faculty interactions appear here. Employment and child care are equally important, another indication of the central non-school roles that compete for the time and energy of older undergraduates. As in the other student models (Figures 3 and 4), coping with stress is a central concern. For this group stress is induced primarily by the need to balance their multiple roles (e.g., worker, family, student) combined with financial strain and concern about the future.

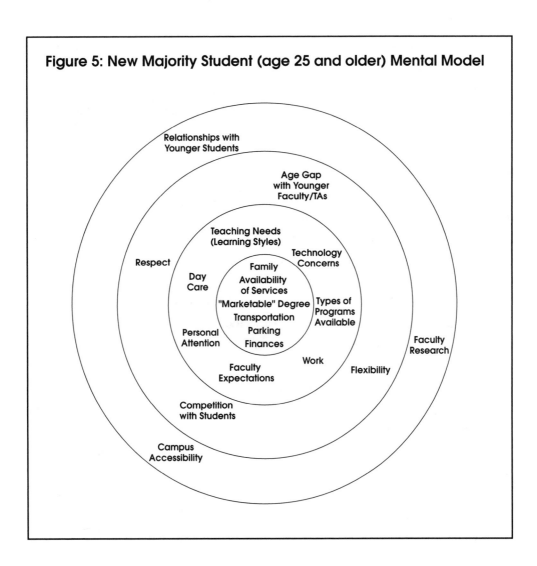

The next ring reflects the relationship between students' life experiences and being accepted by faculty and peers. Many undergraduates over age 25 are established in a job or career and in their local community. At the same time, at many institutions they are surrounded by younger students whose primary role is to study. They are concerned about their writing and reading skills, as they have not attempted academic work for years. For these reasons and others they perceive their status is inconsequential compared with younger students enrolled full-time. Many are preoccupied with earning the respect of professors and peers, and coping with the status issues arising from same- age or younger instructors. In a tight employment market, older students are increasingly perceived by traditional-age students as unwanted competition (Katchadourian & Boli, 1994).

Residence life, the formal co-curriculum, and auxiliary services are all but irrelevant to these students. And, consistent with the two other student mental models, faculty research and allied activities (e.g., publications, grants) are invisible.

Implications

Taken together, the three student mental models suggest that all students view both formal study and personal activities as central to undergraduate education. However, the students' academic focus, in terms of intellectual development and cognitive skills or mastery of a discipline, is somewhat different from that of the faculty. Undergraduates concentrate on the practical value of academic credentials. For this reason, the term "learning" (as the word is used in this monograph) does not appear in the student maps. Students are concerned about classes, grades, and degrees in order to increase their options and enjoy success after college. This conception of academic outcomes is not precisely the same as what the faculty mean by learning.

The other elements appearing in the cores reflect students' purposes for being in college: life transitions, successful vocational preparation, credentials. In the traditional-age student model, peers are prominent in the core and adjacent rings. The focus of life outside the classroom varies from peer relations for residential students to family life and employment for older, commuting undergraduates. Many students focus their non-academic lives on informal campus peer groups, off-campus friends, or family relationships (Moffatt, 1989), essentially oblivious to the formal co-curriculum designed by — or with the help of — student affairs professionals.

The undergraduate models imply that many students are not directly influenced by the services and activities student affairs professionals think are essential. At the same time, students' concerns about accessible services and flexible offerings are not featured in either the faculty or student affairs mental models. For the older students who make up the new majority of undergraduates, many student affairs programs and services have very little to do with their lives and interests. Similarly, faculty scholarship is absent from any undergraduate mental model of learning.

Gender, ethnicity, and family educational background surely influence college experiences and, quite possibly, students' views of learning (Baxter Magolda, 1992;

King, 1996). Although the core elements of each student mental model differs somewhat, all students see their undergraduate experience in terms of their life circumstances and their reasons for attending college. They all see coping with stress as a major challenge, although the sources of the stress vary for different types of students.

WHAT MATTERS TO EXTERNAL STAKEHOLDERS

External constituents are becoming increasingly interested and involved in the internal affairs of colleges and universities. Over the past decade many groups have called for higher education reform (Educational Commission for the States, 1995; The Study Group, 1984; Wingspread Group, 1993). To understand and appreciate these mandates faculty and student affairs professionals must be familiar with what these stakeholders want from colleges and universities with regard to undergraduate education. For this reason we developed a mental model of external stakeholders (Figure 6). Like the mental models of the other groups, the External Stakeholder Mental Model does not encompass all the views of many disparate external groups. Nonetheless, contrasting this model with those of faculty, student affairs professionals, and students provides another useful perspective in understanding what matters in undergraduate education.

Featured in the core of this mental model is preparing students to become productive members of society, which includes vocational training and civic responsibility. The primary venue through which colleges and universities provide students with these skills and competencies is classroom-based instruction (teaching). Activities that complement attainment of these core functions are in the first ring out from the core and reflect student involvement in activities that will give them concrete experience to apply what they are learning in their academic programs, such as internships and community service. Also in this first ring out from the core are activities that ensure appropriate use of institutional and public resources (stewardship) and applied technology which puts knowledge to use. Somewhat less important, in the second ring from the core, are research and development activities that promise to increase the quality of life and other amenities such as cultural, athletic, and recreational events. Also associated with undergraduate education –

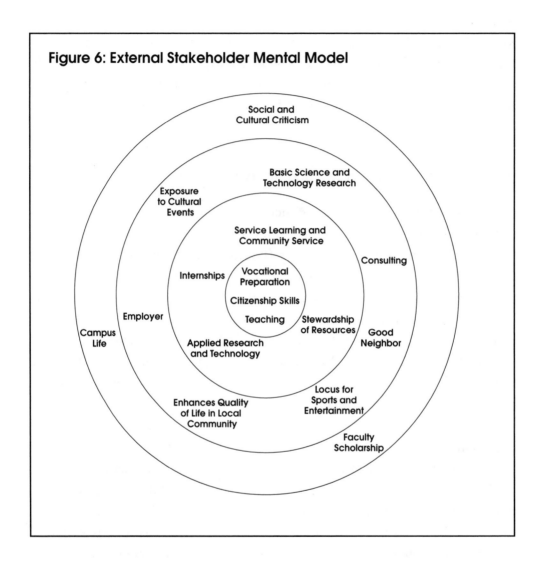

Figure 6: External Stakeholder Mental Model

albeit indirectly—are such matters as providing employment opportunities for people who live nearby (which enhances incomes in the local area) and attracting to the community bright, capable people (including faculty, staff, students) engaged in socially-meaningful activities.

Implications

The external stakeholder's mental model of undergraduate education is most similar to the student models. Although this view acknowledges the value of certain out-of-class activities, it emphasizes those that give students practical skills and those that have entertainment value for a broader audience than just students. This suggests that, for faculty and administrators, communicating to external groups what really matters to undergraduate learning must be a high priority.

COMPARING MENTAL MODELS

Faculty and student affairs professionals ostensibly are working toward the same ends—preparing a college-educated person to be financially self-sufficient and to live an enlightened, satisfying, socially responsible life after college. In their own ways, students and external stakeholders also want these things. But comparing the mental models reveals contradictions in what should be emphasized to attain these goals. No group frames its primary purposes in terms of learning outcomes. Each group puts its interests and priorities at the center, and considers other activities tangential, irrelevant, or contradictory to student learning. Such views contribute to the array of isolated "functional silos" that characterize many colleges and universities (Marchese, 1994)—clusters of academic, student affairs, and other units that have few substantive cross-function contacts, thus blocking opportunities for dialogue and collaboration.

Among the most obvious differences among the models are the competing definitions of learning. The centrality of curriculum in the faculty model indicates that college professors consider learning as intellectual development within the framework of a discipline. Student affairs staff view learning more broadly, considering cognitive growth to be one, but not necessarily the most important, of several interrelated developmental "vectors" (Chickering & Reisser, 1993). Learning is thought to be a developmental process, not a product, such as mastery of a discipline, graduation, or post-degree employment. External stakeholders view learning as preparation for a vocation and civic responsibility.

Some of what faculty members consider to be peripheral educational activities are central to student affairs professionals (Allen & Garb, 1993). Student affairs staff emphasize undergraduates' personal development, social welfare, and out-of-classroom programs and services. As was the case with the faculty's map, the student affairs view highlights the services and activities they oversee: the formal co-curriculum (e.g., organizations, events) and the quality of out-of-class experiences. And student affairs staff also engage in some activities that directly compete with or undermine what faculty are trying to accomplish, such as encouraging students to take on activities that interfere with study time (Allen & Garb, 1993). Finally, given these discrepant starting points, it is not surprising that faculty and student affairs regard each other as occupying separate, often competing turf and that neither fully appreciates the view of external stakeholders.

Some of the differences between the faculty and student affairs views of student learning can be attributed in part to each group's historical and philosophical roots (Allen & Garb, 1993; Caple, 1996). The faculty view reflects the ways in which professors become socialized to their discipline. The German-influenced emphasis on the creation of new knowledge, the increased size and complexity of higher education institutions, and the specialization and departmentalization of academic disciplines were late-19th century developments that have profoundly influenced the roles and identity of the contemporary professoriate (Rudolph, 1962; Vesey, 1965). The gateway to a professorial career is a research-oriented academic degree that requires mastery of a specific discipline and the production of original research in a discipline sub-specialty (Kuh & Whitt, 1988). During and following this training, faculty teach in their field. Many also continue to produce knowledge through research.

In contrast to the German research model, the values and assumptions of the student affairs profession are grounded in a humanistic, "whole person" approach (Caple, 1996; NASPA, 1989), an educational philosophy with roots in the English residential college. This view holds that students' emotional and social development are as important as their intellectual growth in ensuring the goals of individual fulfillment and the common good. Cognitive and affective functioning are thought to be inextricably intertwined (ACPA, 1994; Chickering & Reisser, 1993; Loevinger, 1976), and, in fact, many student affairs professionals believe them to be of equal importance. In many ways this approach is the antithesis to what is valued in the German research model. Some (cf., Allen & Garb, 1993; Bloland, Stamatakos, & Rogers, 1996; Caple, 1996) have argued that, in fact, student affairs professionals have emphasized students' affective development to the neglect of cognitive development, a stance that contributes to the peripheral status of student affairs work within the faculty map.

Neither the faculty nor the student affairs view of undergraduate learning acknowledges the interest of students and external stakeholders in vocational preparation and student preoccupation with informal social life and off-campus commitments. Students tend to be concerned about what might seem to be prosaic matters: fitting in socially, obtaining career credentials, and balancing study, friends, and off-campus responsibilities. In the core of the public's model, too, are pragmatic concerns. At the same time, only the student and the external stakeholder mental models emphasize the salience of post-college careers and connect both academic and non-academic spheres and present and future lives.

Comparing the external stakeholder mental model with faculty and staff models suggests some differences among priorities, if not the substance of activities, of faculty and student affairs professionals. This explains, in part, why tensions and misunderstandings exist between universities and their external constituents. Clearly, a concerted effort is needed to educate the public about the variety of in-class and out-of-class experiences that contribute to a high quality undergraduate experience.

TOWARD A COMMON VIEW OF LEARNING

Although distorted perspectives on the world are illustrated by all the variants of the New York City poster, each city's mindscape makes sense when examined in isolation from the others. However, an authentic map—one produced by a cartographer—portrays cities in relation to one another. Acknowledging the existence of mental models of learning and making them explicit are important steps toward understanding how our visions of learning might impede institutional cooperation on behalf of undergraduates. Analyzing the mental models side by side reveals important differences in what campus groups believe contributes to desired outcomes of the baccalaureate experience. Such conflicting world views are likely to preclude cooperation in creating a seamless undergraduate experience in which students realize the cumulative benefits of complementary undergraduate experiences.

Yet recognizing and discussing mental models — within and among campus groups — and their impact on institutional effectiveness and student learning are not simple tasks. Because mental models are tacit assumptions about "how things work" (Brown, 1997, p. 7) and, also, how things ought to work, seeing them for what they are — only partial maps, not the territory (Weick, 1979) — takes time and commitment. In addition, although we have described mental models here as applicable to, for example, all student affairs professionals, differences also exist within campus groups about "how things work." Student affairs work has been described as a profession in continuing search of agreement about its values and priorities, including what matters in student learning; the challenges involved in seeking any consensus within the field about aspects of our mental maps should not be minimized (Allen & Garb, 1993; Bloland, et al., 1994, 1996; Caple, 1996; Stamatakos & Rogers, 1984; Whitt et al., 1990).

Assuming that all the mental models of learning have been examined and their assumptions tested, campus groups then need to work toward developing a common view of learning, including indices of success. This requires that both faculty and student affairs broaden their definitions of learning by recognizing the importance of tightening the connections between in-class and out-of-class learning, and focusing on students' preoccupations and purposes for higher education. This also suggests that, for colleges and universities to make undergraduate education more effective, campus constituencies need more accurate pictures about the conditions and activities that are associated with student learning. Comparing these models to the research on college outcomes distinguishes myth from reality in terms of the kinds of experiences that contribute to learning and personal development (Pascarella, 1995; Terenzini & Pascarella, 1994).

Mental models can be reoriented to achieve a shared view of learning, but doing so in complex and unpredictable organizations such as colleges and universities (Kuh, Whitt, & Shedd, 1987) will require leadership from the institution's president and other senior officers. In addition to guiding dialogue on institutional mission and goals for learning, presidents can underscore the importance of student learning to institutional planning, regional accreditation self-studies, and institutional research and assessment. Dissemination of student learning principles and research may be incorporated into existing campus efforts to evaluate and improve teaching and academic advising. Senior student affairs and academic affairs staff are particularly important factors in facilitating collaborative consideration of shared visions. Students themselves must actively participate in discussions on what matters to their education. Town meetings, teach-ins, speakers' series, student newspapers, and campus community letters and reports are other institutionalized means of promoting campus dialogue on topics such as student learning. Whenever possible, external stakeholders must be involved in these discussions.

Finally, student affairs professionals need to participate more deeply in the intellectual life of their institution. To cultivate a higher degree of intellectualism among student affairs professionals will require leadership of senior student affairs officers in staff selection, professional staff development, and administrative culture. Also, we suggest that modifications will be required in the student selection process and curricula of graduate preparation programs, as well as changes in what professional organizations value and what occurs at their meetings.

Examples of organizations in which mental models are made explicit and examined in dialogue across and within departments, in order to achieve shared perspectives and enhance productivity, can be found in the growing body of literature about "learning organizations" (cf., Brown, 1997; Senge, 1990; Tinto, 1997). Indeed, "in 'learning organizations,' individuals and teams are increasingly aware of and articulate about the lenses through which they are seeing the world, and the theories they are building about that world" (Brown, 1997, p. 7).

CONCLUSION

A gap has existed for a long time between what student affairs professionals and faculty value and how each group spends their time (Blake, 1979, 1996). At the same time, students and external groups have somewhat different perspectives about what they want as a result of college experiences. Each group's notion of what matters in undergraduate learning is unique; no single vision is shared across constituencies. Each appears locked into mental models that define goals in terms of existing functional areas and preferred activities. Yet, now more than ever, higher education leaders need to rethink old roles and traditional spheres of influence.

Developing a common view of student learning demands that faculty and student affairs staff identify and acknowledge their differing assumptions, values, and beliefs, and work together to find a shared vision of student learning, and what matters in undergraduate education. Within this shared vision, student involvement in educationally purposeful activities and the application of learning across contexts are measures of success for every campus group. Such a commitment fixes attention on undergraduate outcomes instead of organizational structures and functions and preferred activities. Most important, investing the time, energy, and commitment required to develop a shared vision of learning makes students the focus of institutional effort, and engages all members of the community in a collective effort to establish student learning as an institutional imperative. In Chapter 3, Marcia Baxter Magolda addresses the process of reorienting the student affairs "mindscape" by defining and redefining student learning.

Defining and Redefining Student Learning

Marcia Baxter Magolda

> *Why learning occurs is as profound a campus mystery as it was in 1400 . . . Campuses grew up in the first place because scholars congregate around books and students around scholars. You pay to watch someone think. Then they watch you think.*
>
> —Matthews, 1997, p. 203

"Putting student learning first" sounds reasonable enough, if only we could agree what learning is, how it occurs, and who is responsible for it (Caple, 1996). There are numerous theories explaining student learning, as many perspectives on how it happens, and multiple arguments for whose responsibility it is. In Chapter Two, Karen Arnold and George Kuh posited that perhaps the most substantive obstacles to "putting student learning first" in student affairs are our own mental models or constructions of our place in the educational process. In other words, the particular definition of learning or the specific theoretical framework we choose to understand and promote learning may be less important than our ability to view ourselves as central to the learning mission of our colleges and universities. Reorienting the mental models we hold as a profession, therefore, is at the foundation of reconceptualizing the role of student affairs in achieving higher education's learning imperative.

Redesigning the student affairs profession's "mindscape" about what matters in undergraduate education involves at least two primary activities. First, we must reflect on our professional philosophies, values, and assumptions. Second, we need to develop a view of learning consistent with our philosophical foundations, thereby creating a foundation on which to construct learning-oriented practice. This chapter begins with reflection on the profession's holistic learning philosophy originally advanced in the Student Personnel Point of View (NASPA, 1989) and the activity-focused delivery systems that have clouded the learning dimension of that philosophy. I continue by considering the impact of the student development movement on our views of student learning and our role in fostering learning outcomes. I then offer a holistic vision of student learning to contribute to the dialogue surrounding moving toward learning-oriented student affairs practice.

The perspectives in this chapter emerged from the Student Learning Project Work Group's dialogue about the role of student learning in our professional mission. Some of our dialogue is shared here to remind readers that similar discussions are needed in many student affairs contexts in order to construct more productive mental models for our field.

STUDENT AFFAIRS "MINDSCAPES" REVISITED

The guiding assumptions of the student affairs profession were first captured in the *Student Personnel Point of View* (*SPPV*), written in 1937 and revised in 1949. A holistic view of the student was set forth in the 1937 version: "This philosophy imposes upon educational institutions the obligation to consider the student as a whole . . . It puts emphasis, in brief, upon the development of the student as a person rather than upon his (sic) intellectual training alone" (NASPA, 1989, p.49). This philosophy was elaborated in the 1949 version: "The development of students as whole persons interacting in social institutions is the central concern of student personnel work and of other agencies of education . . . The concept of education is broadened to include attention to the students' well-rounded development – physically, socially, emotionally, and spiritually, as well as intellectually" (NASPA, 1989, p. 21-22). These assumptions represent what Young (1996) called the organic values of the profession.

The *SPPV* described functions of student affairs work as the delivery system for these values about education and students. The 1949 *SPPV* listed 17 elements of a student personnel program (e.g., counseling, record-keeping, housing and food services) and connected each function with desired student learning outcomes (called "needs" in the *SPPV*). Unfortunately, over time, these functions in many colleges and universities evolved into a service and support role for student affairs, rather than an educational one (Allen & Garb, 1993; Bloland et al., 1994).

In the mid-1970s the Tomorrow's Higher Education (T.H.E.) Project and other similar efforts advocated a shift in the focus of student affairs work from service to student development (Brown, 1972, 1996). Over the past twenty years, student affairs professionals have been introduced to, and used, theories from a variety of disciplines, including psychology and sociology, to understand the nature of growth and change in college students. Theories of psychosocial, moral, and identity development have contributed a useful framework for research on college students, as well as student affairs practice (Brown, 1996; King & Baxter Magolda, 1996).

Many have argued, however, that another consequence of the "student development movement" was fragmentation of our views of, and work with, students (Allen & Garb, 1993; Bloland et al., 1994, 1996). In a residence hall community, for example, we frame our practice according to theories of psychosocial development. In classroom settings, we are concerned about the student's cognitive and intellectual development. In a judicial hearing, we focus on the student's moral development. Each of the theories can be an appropriate way to think about, and plan for, student learning. Yet this focus on separate aspects of students' development can obscure our view of the student as a whole and complex person.

Other critics of the student development movement assert that we have overemphasized psychosocial development and paid too little attention to students' cognitive growth (Allen & Garb, 1993; Bloland et al, 1994, 1996; Caple, 1996). This emphasis can, it is argued, move us away from the central learning mission of our institutions and toward the margins (or, as described in Chapter Two, the outer rings).

In a 1993 article entitled "Reinventing Student Affairs: Something Old and Something New," Kathleen Allen and Elliot Garb traced the context in which the student affairs profession evolved. They explained how the faculty's increasing specialization and focus on the intellect, the need for control resulting from the growth of bureaucracy, and the assignment of student-related issues to student affairs staff combined to create for the profession a mental model of service despite the guiding assumptions of education in the *SPPV*. This mental model, with its notion of student affairs as secondary and marginal, prompted Allen and Garb (1993) to charge that "we have abdicated our role as active shapers of learning-centered education" (p.97). Their re-invented vision of student affairs entails valuing student affairs perspectives, acting as leaders within institutions, and articulating a vision of holistic development that includes a learning focus. This new mental model recaptures the educational mission and the learning-focused delivery systems initially sketched in the *SPPV*. This reorientation of our mental model views traditional student services functions and roles from a learning orientation rather than the service delivery to which we have become accustomed.

Allen and Garb (1993) closed their essay with an invitation to dialogue. This dialogue, already underway in the profession, was furthered by the *Student Learning Imperative* (ACPA, 1994). As we already have noted in this monograph, the expressed purpose of the *SLI* was to advocate a learning-oriented approach to student affairs work and stimulate further discussion "on how student affairs professionals can intentionally create the conditions that enhance student learning and personal development" (p.1). Charles Schroeder interpreted this perspective on student affairs work as "not conducting business with different labels, but conducting different business" (1996, p.115) in his editorial to introduce the *Journal of College Student Development's* special issue on the *SLI*.

This mental model is far more consistent with the current landscape of higher education. If student affairs is to achieve our — and higher education's — learning imperatives, we must seriously consider transforming our mental models. An excerpt of the Student Learning Project Work Group's efforts to reorient our own mental models of "how things work" into a shared definition of learning is offered next to illustrate the obstacles and possibilities in such an undertaking.

A HOLISTIC VISION OF STUDENT LEARNING

As we began our discussion about the implications for student affairs of the *Student Learning Imperative*, we came quickly to the recognition that we would have to define student learning; what processes and outcomes did we have in mind when we used that phrase? Once we embarked on a dialogue about how to define student learning, we realized that many different mental models and notions about student learning were present, *just* in our small group of twelve professionals. This reinforced for us the difficulties involved in, yet the importance of, examining our multiple definitions of learning and multiple views of "what matters" as a profession in order to come to a shared vision of our work.

We recognized, at length, that a new mental model of student learning had to meaningfully integrate cognitive and affective dimensions and reflect the complex interaction between environment and student development. This dialogue was the context for developing a holistic vision of student learning.

Our definition of student learning rests on the assumption that cognitive, intrapersonal and interpersonal dimensions of learning are inextricably related, and the belief that practical outcomes are a result of integrated learning in all three dimensions. Thus, our vision of learning assumes that distinctions among terms such as personal development, student development, and learning are meaningless, if not destructive (Baxter Magolda, 1996; King & Baxter Magolda, 1996). Fostering student learning in all its complexity requires integration of all domains of learning and involvement of all educators, regardless of their campus role.

The *SLI* identified five hallmarks of educated persons. We decided that these "hallmarks" were too narrow for our purposes and so we reorganized the *SLI* hallmarks into four broad dimensions of learning. These dimensions comprise our definition of student learning: cognitive competence, intrapersonal competence, interpersonal competence, and practical competence. *Cognitive competence* encompasses critical thinking, complex meaning-making, intellectual flexibility, reflective judgment, and the ability to apply knowledge. *Intrapersonal competence* includes a coherent sense of identity; a self-authored belief system to organize one's values, ethics, spirituality and moral development; a capacity for self-awareness and reflection; and integrity. *Interpersonal competence* involves the capacity for interdependence and collaboration; appreciation of diversity; communication, problem solving and conflict-management skills; humanitarianism and concern for the community. *Practical competence* includes managing one's daily life and tasks and career and personal decision making.

Numerous reports and research on the status of higher education could be cited as sources for these dimensions of learning and expectations for students (cf., Levine & Cureton, 1998b; NASULGC, 1997; Wingspread Group, 1993). They agree that college graduates must be able to "use their acquired knowledge to make judgments, to develop critical perspectives . . . and to take responsibility for their thinking." (Baxter Magolda, 1996, p. 17). In addition, a vast literature exists on each dimension, including multiple interpretations of each and multiple understandings of how each occurs. A brief review of key points in this literature follows in Chapter 4.

My purpose here is to convey a holistic definition of student learning that can be used by student affairs professionals to examine and reorient their own mental models of learning, and — more important — to create opportunities and environments for learning on their campuses. Therefore, in the sections that follow, I offer one student's experience (1) to provide practical examples of our dimensions of learning, and (2) to illustrate, in vivid terms, the importance of integrating students' and educators' mental models of what matters in undergraduate education. This student, Al, is a participant in a ten-year longitudinal study of student learning and intellectual development (Baxter Magolda, 1992, 1995, 1996).

AL'S STORY

Al has been a student for most of his life. After four years in college he used his undergraduate marketing degree to obtain a position in computer consulting. During his second year in that line of work, Al began to reconsider his goals, and, as a result, returned to college to take science courses in preparation for a career in medicine. At the time of the conversation reported here, Al was completing his second year in medical school. His experiences and views on learning throughout his seven years in higher education illustrate the integration of cognitive, intrapersonal, interpersonal and practical competence.

The focus of Al's annual interviews in recent years has been life and career decisions. Exploring how these decisions evolved illuminates their underlying cognitive, intrapersonal and interpersonal dimensions. Reflecting on the career decisions he made upon graduation, Al explained:

> The reason I took the job I did was I looked at the long term and said, "Where am I going to be in ten years with this company versus these other companies?" The opportunity for growth with the company I was in is amazing and you can move up fast. If you do a nice job you're going to be making 300 thousand dollars in ten years and you'll have a lot of responsibility. A good thing about the job I had was that they gave me a lot of responsibility right off the bat. I think what I did in college was what I wanted to do and what I

should have done. I wanted to do what I was doing. So my decision
was not, "This is what I think I should do." It was what I thought I
wanted to do. But once [I] got out there, I had a change . . .

Although Al described his first position as what he thought he wanted to do, the
criteria he applied in making that decision were advancement and responsibility,
two values common in the socialization of students in higher education. In fact, he
was given substantial responsibility and *was* promoted quickly. Despite those
successes, he found the job wanting for a number of reasons. His explanation of
what followed this realization illustrates that growth in the intrapersonal and cognitive
dimensions played a central role in his dissatisfaction and his resolution of it.

Intrapersonal Competence

The change Al encountered once he was in the work force began with these thoughts:
After you've worked a year or so, you start to realize you're going to
be working the rest of your life. I don't think that really hits home to
you when you're in college. I mean, you realize you're going to have
to get a job, but you really don't feel what it's all about until you get
out there and do it. After a year, you know, I learned a lot with the
company I worked for. And I didn't dislike it.

Gaining an understanding about his new line of work led Al to consider a number of
desirable job criteria that were not evident in his first career decision. One criterion
was what he was accomplishing in his work:
The biggest thing, though, is what am I really doing? In my job, even
though we helped out a lot of people, I never really felt like it was
the kind of help I wanted to give to people. How I can do a job faster
to me is not as important as helping a kid get through cancer or
something like that. So that's the kind of what I looked at making
the decision.

Al's discovery that he valued helping others in a way that differed from his current
work called into question the value of what he was doing. His values and sense of
ethics also came into play in another way:

> At times I almost felt like I was cheating people, too, in my job. And here I am, a year out of school or whatever, and the company can charge $120 an hour for me to sit in a meeting. And I just feel like I want to spend my life helping people more than just making companies more efficient or something, which is a good thing, but it's just not the kind of good I want to do.

These thoughts reveal that Al's increased intrapersonal competence in the form of defining his own values and ethics affected his view of his work and his vision of what he might do instead. This process illustrates the beginnings of *integrity*: "The first step [in developing integrity] requires clarification of the values to which people are committed and that provide the major organizers for their words and deeds" (Chickering & Reisser, 1993, p. 314).

Al's intrapersonal competence also reflected an increased capacity for *self-awareness and reflection* that was not evident in his earlier decision-making. Al began to look at his volunteer activities, including being a big brother and part of a group to help teen runaways, to define his interests and purpose:

> [Through] volunteer activities I figured out what I looked forward to most, enjoyed most — I loved anything that involved kids . . . Knew I wanted to work with kids- I started to think of careers out there- teacher, social worker, pediatrics. Then I considered what else is important-intellectual challenge, not everybody can go and do well in medical school- I can do that. We need doctors who are in it for the right reasons. I feel I could make a difference- I'm not in it for the money; I want to help kids. It's the best choice for me . . . It's not the only option, but it's the best option. Consider your strengths. How I could have the most impact. What is driving me is feeling- what I feel right about- what I feel is my purpose, what makes me feel good. Some things you have to rule out. Every possibility that is out there that I would enjoy is not an option. That's where rationality comes in.

Al's reflections moved him beyond his earlier definition of success to identification of his core values. At this point, he was engaged in Chickering and Reisser's second step in developing integrity: "achieving congruence and internal consistency between word and word, word and deed, deed and deed" (1993, p. 314). He was able to choose his own beliefs on the basis of his increased self awareness and because he viewed himself as capable of making a judgment based on his context. He was in the process of achieving "an internal identity, a *self-authorship* that can coordinate, integrate, act upon, or invent values, beliefs, convictions, generalizations, ideals, abstractions, interpersonal loyalties, and intrapersonal states" (Kegan, 1994 p. 185, italics in original). Al's progress in intrapersonal competence — his growing sense of identity, a self-authored belief system, his capacity for self-awareness and reflection, and integrity — are integrally related to his simultaneous progress in cognitive competence.

Cognitive Competence

The cognitive competence dimension is evident in Al's self-authorship as well as in his analysis of his career options. As Al sorted through his options, he determined some to be more reasonable than others based on evidence of his strength and purpose. He elaborated:

> You've got to weigh all goals. You can't say, "Well, I love picking apples. So I'm going to be an apple picker." That may make sense in one standpoint, but for other standpoints it doesn't. So it's not as simple as "This is what I want to do, so I'm going to do it." But I think you have to be doing something you want to do or you're never going to be happy. But there's a lot of other jobs that could meet those other criteria that aren't going to meet my criterion of "This is what I enjoy doing." So you've got to try to meet as many of those, I think, as you can. . . So it's more complicated than I guess I made it sound initially.

Al's thinking reflects the contextual knower's (Baxter Magolda, 1992) perspective that knowledge claims in an uncertain world are possible in the context of relevant evidence. His *intellectual complexity* and *flexibility* are inherent in decision making based on changing evidence. As his understanding of himself and his values has increased, he makes new decisions about his future.

Thus, Al's intrapersonal and cognitive competence combined to lead him to a purpose with which he was comfortable. He described its importance in his life:

> For me I need to have a purpose. I'm trying to achieve something.
> It adds something to my life . . . The key issue for anybody is feeling
> good about what you are doing. It has impact on other aspects of
> life for me – people have seen a change in me since I have started
> on this path. I think everyone searches for it; some aren't willing to
> take the risk to do it, then never reach it . . . Happiness and mental
> health is having a purpose – goals, feeling like you are accomplishing
> and helping.

Al's *complex meaning-making* is evident in the way he thinks about possible options. He is integrating vocational plans, personal interests, and interpersonal interests – the major elements of developing purpose (Chickering and Reisser, 1993, p. 212). He is increasingly "guided by his own vision" (Kegan, 1994, p. 172) and his vision is constantly becoming more clear.

Al's ability to *acquire knowledge* and *apply it* in new contexts helped him pass the MCAT examination for medical school. He offered this interpretation of his experience:

> MCAT's were tough. I had very few courses that applied; the bare
> minimum to get in medical school . . . I studied three months, reading,
> looking at notes. There were things on there I had never seen . . . I
> guessed the right answer a lot . . . I knew what it wasn't, based on
> similar things I've seen. May be a skill for that—inductive reasoning.

Al's ability to make judgments within contexts is crucial to his success in medical school. Processing his first year, he offered:

> The material isn't hard—anybody could learn it. The volume is
> difficult . . . It's like trying to drink out of a fire hose. Sheer volume.
> You have to be selective to figure out what you need to learn. I started
> off really wanting to learn as opposed to figuring out what I needed
> for a certain score. This is my life now. I need to know it. It is almost
> impossible to do that. I had to shift back to efficiency mode—figure
> out what I'll be tested on, as opposed to really learn and understand
> . . . I'm forgetting things that I'll need; have to learn it for boards
> anyway. . . I was usually in the top of the class in undergraduate and
> premed. I'm in the top 15% now, a new perspective for me. I realize

there are other things to get involved in . . .Those things are more
important to me than being number 1 or 2 in the class.

Although Al was disappointed in the prevalent approach to learning in medical school,
he accepted it as reality and made judgments about how to succeed. He gave up
"really learning and understanding" to the extent necessary to pass his courses,
rationalizing that the knowledge he needed would be recovered when he studied for
his "boards." Al's contextual perspective and ability to employ reflective thinking
mediate how he acquires and applies information. His cognitive competence –
complex meaning-making, critical thinking, intellectual flexibility, reflective
judgment, and ability to acquire and apply knowledge – is employed in the service of
his intrapersonal values as well as in the context of his interpersonal competence,
discussed next.

Interpersonal Competence

Al's interpersonal competence also is woven through the recent evolution of his career
and life. Al's *concern for community* and *humanitarianism* were evident before he began
to connect them to career decisions. Since leaving college, Al had been involved in a
big brother program. He talked about its effect on his life:

I'm a Big Brother. I have a "little brother"; I've had him for two years
now . . . We still do stuff almost every week. Every time we do
something I can just feel like I can be kind of a role model or give
him that male perspective of things that he doesn't get. His Mom
does a great job; I really respect her. We have a great time. His mother's
told me a few times how much a difference it has made in this kid.
So that really makes me feel good about that.

The satisfaction Al experienced in interacting with his "little brother" struck him as
more fun than his college activities and, at the same time, a contribution. Al had
moved away from involvement in church during college; he stated he had allowed
fraternity life to steer him away from what he knew was right. As he became active in
his church after college, Al felt called to do "good" for other people. He exchanged
his dependence on his fraternity peers during college for interdependence and
collaboration with others in his volunteer activities.

The settings Al frequented as a result of his humanitarian values required *communication, problem-solving* and *conflict management* skills. As a Project Safe Place volunteer, for example, he was responsible for picking up runaway teens who had contacted the shelter and helping them decide on a course of action. Building projects and planning activities for his church group also required these skills.

Al described some of his progress on interpersonal competence as stemming from his consulting work. He was often frustrated when decisions were made to do things in ways he thought were not the best options. He reported:

> I had to take a step back and try to open myself up to more ideas and more ways of doing things. And then if I still think the way I would normally do it is the best, I have had to learn to roll with whatever we came up with or whatever was decided. That's something I have struggled with. But I'm working on it. I'm still struggling with it, but I think it's making me a better person for it.

Al was learning how to *collaborate* and *work interdependently* with others. He also was making progress on *appreciating diversity*. Kegan (1994) noted that one of the demands of us as citizens in a diverse society is to "resist our tendencies to make 'right' or 'true' that which is merely familiar, and 'wrong' or 'false' that which is only strange" (p. 302). Al's openness to new ideas, both in his work and volunteer activities, aided his interpersonal competence. Much of his motivation to gain interpersonal competence stemmed from the intrapersonal and cognitive competence described earlier.

Practical Competence

We hope that college graduates will be able to manage their daily lives and tasks in order to meet their personal, work, and social responsibilities. This entails defining priorities, balancing conflicting interests, developing discipline to devote energy to necessary tasks, and managing time effectively. After graduation, Al acquired a job, moved to a new city, and rented an apartment. He was able to manage his everyday tasks as well as function successfully at work, a particular challenge as his job required skills and understanding beyond his undergraduate preparation. In this context he was also able to engage in volunteer work, suggesting that his time management skills were already in place. Upon leaving this position after two years, Al was able to manage his finances to pay for undergraduate courses and acquire a second consulting job to help pay for medical school while he waited to begin.

Summary

Having a clear sense of himself and his goals (intrapersonal dimension), a self-authored system of making judgments (cognitive dimension), and a vision of how he wants to interact with others (interpersonal dimension) have enabled Al to develop practical competence in a relatively stressful situation. He is succeeding in medical school, no small feat, but, he also is taking advantage of additional opportunities for practical experience as he shadows doctors and works in clinics. He was selected to a committee by his peers to aid impaired medical students. He maintains his relationship with his little brother, plays sports with friends, and stays involved in his church activities.

DEFINING AND REDEFINING LEARNING FOR STUDENT AFFAIRS

The definition of student learning described here incorporates all the aspects of students' experiences with which student affairs has always been concerned. Helping students identify their values, understand themselves, and learn how to act accordingly are essential aspects of our role as educators. Challenging students to think for themselves, identify and commit to their beliefs, and integrate those beliefs into their lives has been a long-standing goal of student affairs professionals. Teaching students collaboration, communication, problem-solving, and conflict management skills to heighten their capacity for interdependence is a mainstay of student affairs work. Coaching students in life management, time management, and decision-making skills is evident in most student affairs activities. Integration of students' learning about themselves, their disciplines, and the world of work has been the foundation for supporting their career and personal development. Thus, the holistic view of student learning we advocate here returns student affairs to its philosophical roots.

If this is a return to what we already believe, then what is different? If these activities reflect the historical mission of student affairs work, why has implementing the *Student Learning Imperative* been described as "not conducting business with different labels, but conducting different business" (Schroeder, 1996, p.115). As I noted earlier in this chapter, despite our historical and philosophical commitments, a strong case can be made that student affairs professionals have become preoccupied with their functions, programs, and practices without questioning the assumptions and purposes — the mental models — that shape those activities. The extent to which student learning — clearly and holistically defined — undergirds and guides decisions about how student affairs professionals spend their time (and do not spend their time) is, I would argue, largely unexamined. In the process, some aspects of student affairs work have maintained a focus on learning while others have become ends in themselves (Allen & Garb, 1996; Schroeder, 1996).

For example, the requirement that Resident Assistants "program" for or with their residents a certain number of times each semester is common at most residential campuses. Those programs usually are referred to as "educational" and they often are used as an example of the ways in which residence halls complement or support the academic mission of the institution. Yet, to what extent are the programs designed to achieve specific learning outcomes? To what extent is their educational impact assessed? Or to what extent have they become routine and unquestioned expectations? Evidence from research on the impact of out-of-class environments and activities is clear: the contributions of residence hall experiences to student learning depend *not* on the place of residence (e.g., does a student live on campus or off?), but on the ways in which those experiences "blur the boundaries between students' academic and out-of-class lives" (Terenzini et al., 1996, p. 158) and make clear connections between in-class and out-of-class learning (Kuh et al., 1994).

Our challenge as a profession, then, is to examine our current "mental models" of student learning, as well as of the roles and priorities of student affairs professionals, and determine whether they help or hinder acting on our student learning imperative. A holistic vision of student learning includes student affairs at the center of higher education's effort to "put student learning first," and opens the way for our active participation in addressing the important challenges our institutions face. To make the most of the opportunities this vision creates, student affairs — as a profession and as individuals — must articulate how current student affairs roles and activities foster student learning (as well as how some must be reorganized and reshaped to do so) and how we can work with academic colleagues to develop seamless learning environments for all students (Kuh, 1996, 1998). Chapters Five and Six in this monograph address these tasks in more detail.

One aspect of student affairs work that should not change is our concern for students. Some student affairs staff have wondered whether focusing on student learning will overshadow our long-standing commitment to care for and about students. To the contrary, the holistic vision of learning described here implies — at the most basic level — a caring approach. In fact, many experts (e.g., Baxter Magolda, 1992; Belenky, Clinchy, Goldberger and Tarule, 1986; Noddings, 1991; Palmer, 1990) have described learning as a relational activity, requiring interactions between educators and students similar to the caring relationships that have been central to student affairs work.

CONCLUSION

This chapter began with a question and a lament: how can we put student learning first if we cannot agree what learning is and who is responsible for making sure it occurs? The holistic definition and vision of student learning described here is one way to think about "what learning is" that reflects the complex ways students change and develop in college. And, inherent in this definition, is an answer to the second question. Who is responsible for making sure learning occurs? All of us.

CHAPTER 4

Student Learning Outside the Classroom: What Does the Research Tell Us?

Elizabeth J. Whitt • *Thomas E. Miller*

In Chapter 3, Marcia Baxter Magolda defined student learning in terms of categories of college outcomes. Those categories serve here as a framework for an overview of research on student learning outside the classroom. The purpose for this review is twofold: (1) to provide the reader with some basic information about the contributions of learning environments outside the classroom to desired learning outcomes, and (2) to provide a context for our discussions about assessment and action plans for creating learning-oriented student affairs divisions.

Before proceeding, however, we must offer two caveats. First, this review is, by necessity, brief and simple. There is much more research, and the results of the research are much more complex, than this review might imply. We have drawn heavily on what we believe are the very best resources, including Alexander Astin's (1993) research on what matters in college, Pascarella and Terenzini's (1991) synthesis of research on how college affects students, a description of out-of-class influences on cognitive development by Terenzini, Pascarella, and Blimling (1996), and a review by Kuh, Branch Douglas, Lund, and Ramin-Gyurnik (1994) of research on student learning outside the classroom. These and other important works — with which student affairs professionals should be familiar — are identified in the reference list at the end of the monograph.

Second, we have chosen to focus on research on student learning outside the classroom with the knowledge that this can, in many ways, perpetuate an inappropriate and undesirable bifurcation of students' experiences. We know that distinctions such as "curricular" and "co-curricular," "academic" and "non-academic" do not reflect the holistic ways in which students learn. At the same time, however, it is essential that student affairs practitioners know how out-of-class experiences and environments influence students' learning; such knowledge is needed to inform policies, practices, and programs and to demonstrate the contributions of student affairs to educational outcomes.

The review begins with an overview and critique of the design of studies of student learning, including research methods and data sources. The chapter concludes with a summary of the research results and their implications for student affairs.

RESEARCH DESIGN

Research Methods

Most of the research on student learning in college has been conducted with quantitative methods (Pascarella & Terenzini, 1991). That is, the data are numbers, and most have been collected by means of questionnaires or surveys administered at a single point in time. Most of these studies rely on students' self-reports of learning and gains in college (e.g., Kuh, Pace, & Vesper, 1997). Only a few studies, such as the National Study of Student Learning (cf, Pascarella, E.T., Edison, M.I., Nora, A., Hagedorn, L.S., & Terenzini, P.T., 1998; Pascarella, Whitt, Nora, Edison, Hagedorn, & Terenzini, 1996; Whitt, E.J., Edison, M.I., Pascarella, E.T., Nora, A., & Terenzini, P.T., in press) have used objective, standardized tests (e.g., the Collegiate Assessment of Academic Proficiency (CAAP), developed by the American College Testing Program (American College Testing Program, 1991), to measure learning over time. For an excellent review of the strengths and limitations of quantitative methods for studying student learning, see Pascarella and Terenzini (1991) and Pascarella (1991).

Qualitative methods, research in which the data are words and have been collected and analyzed by the researcher (Whitt, 1991), have been used infrequently to study student learning. A few studies, such as the College Experiences Study (Kuh et al., 1991), Marcia Baxter Magolda's (1992) work on epistemological development, and research about students' college experiences by Robert Rhoads (1994; 1995a; 1995b), Peter Magolda (1997), and Michael Moffatt (1989) are notable exceptions. Although these studies provide vivid descriptions of students and their learning environments, largely told in the students' voices, the complicated nature of qualitative research — especially on a topic as complex as learning — can be daunting.

Another form in which research on student learning takes is syntheses or meta-analyses. Pascarella and Terenzini's (1991) book *How College Affects Students* is perhaps the most well-known and most thorough of these studies. Syntheses offer not only a wealth of information about research conducted on a particular topic, they provide a means to examine the nature and implications of an entire body of knowledge.

Data Sources

Data sources for research on college student outcomes are varied, although most such research has been conducted in single institutions (Pascarella & Terenzini, 1991). These studies are, for the most part, the result of institutional research efforts, such as to address a concern about retention, or specific interests of faculty, staff, or graduate students. The generalizability of these studies to other settings should be a concern for the reader, even when single-institution studies can be combined into a body of work on a particular topic, such as moral development (Pascarella, 1997a).

College impact also has been studied across institutions. Examples of such studies, include the aforementioned National Study of Student Learning (Pascarella et al., 1996) and the College Experiences Study (Kuh et al., 1991). Some multi-institution studies use and/or generate large national data bases, such as the Cooperative Institutional Research Program/Higher Education Research Institute (at UCLA) (Astin, 1993) and the College Student Experiences Questionnaire (cf., Kuh et al., 1997; Pace, 1990).

Limitations

Extant research on college outcomes has a number of limitations of which the reader should be aware. Useful detailed discussions of these limitations can be found in Pascarella and Terenzini (1991), Pascarella (1991), and Pascarella and Terenzini (1998). These limitations can, however, be summarized as "who," "why," and "how." Limitations regarding "who": most research on college impact has been conducted with traditional-age students — primarily Caucasian — in residence at 4-year colleges and universities. As a consequence, the students and institutions that comprise the majority of United States postsecondary education have not been studied (Pascarella & Terenzini, 1998). There is a small, but growing, body of research on first-generation college students and students of color (cf., London, 1996; Rendon, 1996), though much more is needed. Other issues that need further study include experiences of community college students (Pascarella, 1997b) and students with physical disabilities (Hitchings, Luzzo, Retish, Horvath & Ristow, 1998).

As we noted earlier in the chapter, there also are methodological limitations to the research on college impact. Most of this research has been conducted with quantitative methods, at single institutions, at a single point in time (Pascarella, 1991). Our knowledge about outcomes would be enhanced greatly by studies of students across their years in college and across institutions (Pascarella & Terenzini, 1998). Perhaps more important, the usefulness of the research is likely to improve if students are allowed to describe their learning in their own words (Magolda, 1997; Williams, 1997, 1998).

The "why" limitation of the college outcomes research is related to the "how." That is, correlational studies using quantitative methods can tell us what happens, but not always why — at least not in the depth or with the level of internal validity often necessary to help in the formulation of effective policies and practices. For example, recent studies of the impact of student peers on cognitive outcomes provide information about the types of encounters that enhance and inhibit learning (Whitt et al., 1999a, 1999b). But more detailed accounts are needed of how students decide what peers (individuals as well as groups) will influence them, how those influences occur and with what effect.

Finally, the research can be effective only if it is applied to real-world problems. Thus, what is, perhaps, the greatest limitation of the research on student learning is not, in fact, a limitation of the research, but rather of we who — for a variety of reasons — ignore it. Some have argued that there is a large gap between what student affairs professionals say about the value and importance of research to their work and the extent to which such research actually is used (Brown, 1991; Whitt & Pascarella, 1999). The use of inquiry is, in fact, "the missing ingredient" (Erwin, 1996, p. 416) in much student affairs practice. No matter what explanations or excuses for not using research on student learning are offered (e.g., "I'm too busy to read journals."), none is completely rational or justified in the face of demands that student affairs divisions demonstrate their effectiveness and their contributions to student learning (ACPA, 1994; Erwin, 1996; Guskin, 1994; Kuh, 1998).

SUMMARY OF RESULTS OF RESEARCH ON STUDENT LEARNING OUTSIDE THE CLASSROOM

Outcomes Studied

Research on student learning outside the classroom can be divided into the categories of learning described in the previous chapter: cognitive competence, intrapersonal competence, interpersonal competence, and practical competence. Cognitive competence includes such outcomes as critical thinking, intellectual flexibility, reflective judgment, complex meaning-making, reasoning, comprehension, and independent judgment (ACPA, 1994; Kuh et al, 1994). Intrapersonal competence comprises, among other things, capacity for self-awareness, self-reflection, an integrated identity, and a self-authored belief system (Kuh et al, 1994; Baxter Magolda, 1992). Interpersonal competence includes collaboration, communication, problem-solving, conflict management, concern for community, and effectiveness with diversity (ACPA, 1994; Kuh et al, 1994). Among the outcomes included in practical competence are accomplishing daily tasks, time management, career decision-making, and effective independent action (ACPA, 1994; Kuh et al, 1994). In the following sections, we provide a very brief summary of research on the influence of out-of-class experiences in each of these areas.

Experiences Associated with Gains in Cognitive Competence

Although research on college impact — especially with regard to out-of-class and nonacademic experiences — has tended to focus on psychosocial outcomes, there is an increasing body of work on cognitive and intellectual development (Terenzini et al., 1996). This research includes studies of influences on cognitive development such as interactions with peers (e.g., Astin, 1993; Baxter Magolda, 1992; Kuh, 1995; Kuh et al., 1994; Kuh et al., 1997; Pascarella, Edison, Nora, et al., 1996; Pascarella, Edison, Whitt, et al., 1996; Pascarella, Whitt, et al., 1996; Rhoads, 1994; 1995a; 1995b; Whitt et al., 1999a), interactions with faculty (e.g., Astin, 1993; Baxter Magolda, 1992; Kuh et al., 1994; Pascarella & Terenzini, 1991; Terenzini et al, 1995), participation in clubs and organizations (e.g., Astin, 1993; Kuh, 1995; Kuh et al.,

1991; Kuh et al., 1994; Pascarella, Edison, Whitt, et al., 1996; Pascarella et al., 1997), participation in social fraternities and sororities in the first year of college (e.g., Pascarella, Edison, Whitt, et al., 1996; Pascarella, Whitt, et al., 1996), on- and off-campus employment (e.g., Astin, 1993; Pascarella et al., 1998), experiences with diversity and other campus climate issues (e.g., Pascarella, Edison, Nora, et al., 1996; Pascarella et al., 1997; Whitt et al., 1999a, 1999b), learning communities (Tinto & Goodsell, 1993; Tinto, Goodsell-Love, & Russo, 1993;), and on- and off-campus residence (e.g., Astin, 1993; Blimling, 1993; Inman & Pascarella, in press; Pascarella, Bohr, Nora, Zusman, Inman, & Desler, 1993).

Some aspects of students' out-of-class experience that are, according to these and other studies, associated with gains in cognitive competence (e.g., Astin, 1993; Kuh et al., 1994; Pascarella & Terenzini, 1991; Terenzini et al., 1996) include:

1. student-faculty interaction (when/where students perceive faculty to be concerned with students and teaching, and when/where students have an important relationship with a faculty member; the nature of the interaction that has impact depends on student's stage of development);

2. involvement in a learning community (issue: not where, but what — what sorts of experiences are provided to reinforce in-class learning, apply academic experiences outside the classroom?);

3. involvement in campus clubs and organizations;

4. "balanced" academic and social involvement ("balanced" meaning not too much of either; in fact, the two together have greater impact than each does alone);

5. fraternity membership for African American men;

6. attending racial/cultural awareness workshop;

7. involvement with diverse peers;

8. environments characterized by non-discriminatory attitudes;

9. involvement with peers in course-related activities, including studying with others, talking with others about ideas presented in class, explaining course material to another student, studying with other students in the residence hall; and

10. involvement with peers in non-course-related activities, including talks about art, music, theater; serious discussions with students of different religions, philosophies of life, political opinions or countries of origin; lively conversations over dinner in the cafeteria; late-night "bull sessions."

Experiences Associated with Gains in Interpersonal Competence

Research on influences on interpersonal competence includes studies about leadership (e.g., Astin, 1993; Kuh, 1995; Romano, 1995; Whitt, 1994), volunteer service (e.g., Astin, 1993; Evanoski, 1988; Pascarella & Terenzini, 1991), living in campus residence halls (e.g., Berger, 1997; Pike, Schroeder, & Berry, 1997), student activism (e.g., Rhoads, 1997), and campus employment (e.g., Astin, 1993; Pascarella & Terenzini, 1991). Aspects of students' out-of-class experience that are, according to these and other studies, associated with gains in interpersonal competence (e.g., Astin, 1993; Kuh et al., 1994; Pascarella & Terenzini, 1991; Terenzini et al., 1996) include:

1. involvement in a volunteer service organization;
2. social leadership roles;
3. paraprofessional experiences (e.g., Resident Assistant);
4. interaction with faculty outside the classroom (e.g., discussions with faculty, undergraduate research assistantship, visiting faculty member's home);
5. living on campus, especially in a living-learning residence; and
6. interaction with persons of different races/ethnic backgrounds and of diverse perspectives.

Experiences Associated with Gains in Intrapersonal Competence

Research on influences on intrapersonal competence includes studies on such topics as relationships with roommates (e.g., Fuller & Hall, 1996; Phelps, Altschul, Wisenbaker, Day, Cooper, & Potter, 1998), interactions with diverse peers (e.g., Astin, 1993; Jones, 1997; Kuh, 1995; Mather & Winston, 1998; Poindexter-Cameron & Robinson, 1997), involvement in clubs and organizations (e.g., Astin, 1993; Evanoski, 1988; Kuh, 1995), and study abroad (Kauffman & Kuh, 1985). Aspects of students' out-of-class experience that are, according to these and other studies, associated with gains in intrapersonal competence (e.g., Astin, 1993; Kuh et al., 1994; Pascarella & Terenzini, 1991; Terenzini et al., 1996) include:

1. involvement in leadership roles;
2. interactions with diverse peers and faculty;
3. study abroad; and
4. involvement in student organizations.

Experiences Associated with Gains in Practical Competence

Research on influences on practical competence includes studies on such topics as interactions with faculty (e.g., Astin, 1993), leadership and involvement in clubs, organizations, and service activities (e.g., Astin, 1993; Kuh, 1995; Kuh & Lund, 1994), on- or off-campus employment (e.g., Kuh, 1995; Luzzo, McWhirter, & Hutcheson, 1997; Pascarella & Terenzini, 1991), and institutional type and climate (e.g., Pascarella, Edison, Nora, Hagedorn, & Terenzini, 1998a). Aspects of students' out-of-class experience that are, according to these and other studies, associated with gains in practical competence (e.g., Astin, 1993; Kuh et al., 1994; Pascarella & Terenzini, 1991; Terenzini et al., 1996) include:

1. volunteer involvement;
2. leadership roles;
3. involvement in clubs and organizations;
4. work on or off campus (especially when related to major/goals); and
5. informal interactions with faculty.

Experiences Associated With Negative Outcomes

Anyone who works with college students knows that not all out-of-class experiences are positive. It is important to note, therefore, that some research on college outcomes has demonstrated negative influences on student learning and development (Astin, 1993; Kuh, et al., 1994; Pascarella, Edison, Nora, et al., 1996; Pascarella, Edison, Whitt, et al., 1996; Pascarella, Whitt, et al., 1996; Terenzini et al., 1996), including:

1. fraternity and sorority membership in the first year of college (e.g., Pascarella, Edison, Whitt, et al., 1996; Pascarella, Whitt, et al., 1996);
2. women's perceptions of a 'chilly campus climate' for women (e.g., Pascarella et al., 1997; Whitt et al., 1999b);

3. excessive socializing — academic and social activities out of balance (e.g., Astin, 1993; Terenzini et al., 1995);

4. alcohol and other drug abuse (e.g., Astin, 1993; Pascarella & Terenzini, 1991; Terenzini et al., 1995; Wechsler, 1996, 1997);

5. excessive TV-watching (e.g., Astin, 1993); and

6. intercollegiate football and basketball for men (Pascarella et al, 1995; Pascarella, Whitt, et al., 1996; Pascarella, Truckenmiller, Nora, Terenzini, Edison, & Hagedorn, in press).

SUMMARY OF THE RESEARCH ON STUDENT LEARNING

So, what does the research tell us about the impact of out-of-class experiences on student learning? The reviews and syntheses on which this chapter is based (Astin, 1993; Kuh, et al., 1994; Pascarella & Terenzini, 1991; Terenzini et al., 1996) provide the following conclusions:

Conclusion #1: Out-of-class experiences are important for achieving learning outcomes.

Indeed, according to Terenzini, Pascarella, and Blimling (1996), these experiences are far more important for students' cognitive development than most faculty and others have believed.

Conclusion #2: Some out-of-class experiences have a negative impact on desired learning outcomes.

Conclusion #3: Students *do* learn by being involved.

Astin's theory of involvement (Astin. 1993; 1984) is supported — repeatedly — in this research: engagement is the key. In virtually all cases where out-of-class experiences enhanced learning, the experiences required active student involvement and responsibility, such as for organizing, planning, implementing, and reflecting on what was learned.

Conclusion #4: Students learn from other people.

> The most powerful source of influence on student learning appears to be students' interpersonal interactions, whether with peers or faculty (and, one suspects, staff members)… If one reviews the positive out-of-class influences on student learning listed earlier (e.g., living on campus, working on campus, discussing racial or ethnic issues, having an internship), it is clear that these activities bring students together with their peers or faculty members in situations with the potential for students to encounter new ideas and people different from themselves (Terenzini et al., 1996, p. 158).

And those interactions that discouraged encounters with new ideas and differences, inhibited learning (Pascarella, Edison, Nora, et al., 1996; Pascarella, Edison, Whitt, et al., 1996; Pascarella, Whitt, et al., 1996; Terenzini et al., 1996).

Conclusion #5: Learning experiences are cumulative and interrelated.

That is, "a majority of important changes that occur during college are probably the cumulative result of a set of interrelated experiences sustained over an extended period of time." (Pascarella & Terenzini, 1991, p. 610). Thus, it is unlikely that any one program or policy or activity will affect learning to the extent that a variety of educationally-purposeful experiences in an array of settings over a student's time in college will (Kuh et al., 1991; Kuh et al., 1994).

IMPLICATIONS FOR STUDENT AFFAIRS PRACTICE

Detailed discussions of implications of research on student learning outside the classroom can be found elsewhere (e.g., Kuh et al., 1991; Kuh et al., 1994; Terenzini et al., 1996), however, we can identify at least four implications for student affairs practice here. First, in summarizing their extensive review of research on student learning outside the classroom, Kuh et al. (1994) asserted "the single most important thing that institutional agents can do to enhance student learning is to get students to think more often about what they are doing — in classes and in other areas of their lives — and to apply what they are learning to both" (p. 95). Therefore, "the key task is for student affairs in partnership with the faculty to couple more tightly the connections between the curriculum and out of class life" (Kuh et al., 1994, p. 84). This means that student affairs staff must engage students in thinking about what they are learning and ask them routinely to use that learning in out-of-class activities. This means, too, that student affairs staff must know what students are learning in class and must know and understand the academic goals, requirements, and experiences of the institution. When did you last ask a student what courses she is taking and what she is learning in them?

Second, research on student learning outside the classroom also emphasizes the need to create a learning-oriented campus culture (Terenzini et al., 1996). The learning-oriented student affairs divisions identified in the *Student Learning Imperative* (ACPA, 1994) and described elsewhere in this monograph are essential aspects of such a culture. For example, "whenever a decision is to be made, the learning-centered administrator will ask: 'What will be the likely effect of my choosing this alternative (vs. any other) on our students' learning? Student learning will be the better for such an approach" (Terenzini et al., 1996, p. 159).

Third, learning environments and experiences should enhance the positive effects of students' interactions and minimize the negative effects. Recall that interactions that contribute to learning are encounters with difference — such as with peers from different backgrounds and in discussions that question previously-held beliefs. And recall that interactions that inhibit learning allow students to avoid differences. Consider, for example, the extent to which you challenge the students with whom you work to look at their world from diverse perspectives.

Fourth, student affairs staff should conduct research and assessments about student learning (e.g., learning outcomes; experiences associated with gains and negative effects; learning environments; nature of learning for different students and different environments) on their own campuses and use this research to examine programs, policies, practices. The research reviewed in this chapter and in the other sources we have cited identify outcomes to study, suggest theoretical frameworks to use in designing research, and offer examples of effective approaches for campus-based studies.

CONCLUSION

In this chapter, we have reviewed some of the research on student learning outside the college classroom. The studies demonstrated the value of out-of-class experiences for learning, and reinforce the importance of other people and the quality of student involvement in achieving desired outcomes. The research also reminds us that some out-of-class experiences have a negative influence students and their learning, and that the impact of any single program or activity is not as important as the cumulative effect of environments and experiences across a student's time in college.

These studies — taken together — offer yet another set of challenges to student affairs professionals. First, they remind us to keep abreast of relevant research, and use that research in every aspect of our work with students. Second, they call for a broadening and deepening of the ways in which we think about, and accomplish, our work, so that we can identify additional means by which we foster student learning. Finally, they challenge us to assess current practices to ensure that we have the positive impact we desire. In the next chapter, Ernest Pascarella and Lee Upcraft offer suggestions for creating effective assessments in student affairs.

CHAPTER 5

Assessment Strategies for the Student Learning Imperative

Ernest T. Pascarella • *M. Lee Upcraft*

> *Surely if staff are busy, doing what they have always done, something worthwhile is happening. Or is it?*
>
> —Kuh, 1998, p. 18

There is no doubt that if the *Student Learning Imperative (SLI)* (ACPA, 1994) is to have an impact on student affairs practice, as well as on student learning, the question, "Is something worthwhile happening?" must be answered. Recall that the *SLI* asserted "…if learning is the primary measure of institutional productivity by which the quality of undergraduate education is determined, what and how much students learn also must be the criterion by which the value of student affairs is judged" (1994, p.2). Thus, "Is something worthwhile happening?" can be rephrased: "What and how much are students learning from our student affairs staff, programs, services? And how do we know?" These questions can be answered accurately only with evidence obtained through intentional and systematic assessment.

This chapter discusses implications of the *SLI* for assessment of student affairs activities and practices. We describe why assessment is absolutely essential to higher education and student affairs today, provide some definitions to frame the discussion, suggest several approaches to assessment in student affairs, and offer one example of a research design which assesses the influence of one particular student affairs program on desired student learning outcomes.

WHY ASSESSMENT IN HIGHER EDUCATION AND STUDENT AFFAIRS?

When the assessment movement in higher education first gained momentum in the 1970s, there were many who thought it was yet another fad that would quickly fade from the scene. They were wrong. In the 1980s, several national reports within higher education (e.g., Study Group on Conditions of Excellence in Higher Education, 1984) called for a greater emphasis on assessment in higher education. As Andreas and Schuh noted in Chapter One, in the 1990s, tough questions are being asked about the effectiveness and productivity of colleges and universities.

Many factors have contributed to the current press for assessment. First, there are too many examples of people with college degrees who do not appear to be educated, even in the most basic sense of that term: graduates who are unable to read, write, compute, or do anything else indicative of an educated person. Second, the public is increasingly dissatisfied because of the rising costs of higher education, and the question being asked is, "Is it worth it?" Third, there is increasing dissatisfaction with the quality of instruction at many institutions, including large classes, fewer faculty who actually teach, poor academic advising, failure to do anything about poor teaching, and so forth. Fourth, and no less important, are issues of access and equity in higher education, including the alarming discrepancy between the success rates of members of traditionally-underrepresented groups and those of the majority. And finally, assessment is now required as part of regional accreditation processes (Upcraft & Schuh, 1996).

In sum, the forces that have led to a focus on student learning also have created pressure on colleges and universities to be accountable for achieving learning outcomes (NASULGC, 1997; Wingspread Group, 1993), including demonstrating "the appropriate levels and forms of student learning that occur as a result of the undergraduate education we offer" (Guskin, 1997, p. 4). We need to be able to show that the desired student learning occurs *and* that the people, curricula, programs, and services in our institutions contribute to that learning.

There is a great deal of evidence that this pressure on colleges and universities to demonstrate higher education does what it claims to do, and to provide evidence that it is done efficiently and effectively will not go away — nor should it (Banta & Associates, 1993; Banta, Lund, Black, & Oblander, 1996; Guskin, 1994a, 1994b; Terenzini, 1989; Upcraft & Schuh, 1996). And, as a consequence, programs, services, and activities that fail to implement effective assessment processes and/or fail to demonstrate specific contributions to the educational mission of the institution place themselves in jeopardy (Guskin, 1994a, 1994b; Terenzini, 1989; Upcraft & Schuh, 1996). Therefore, to matters of accountability, cost, quality, access, equity, and accreditation, is added survival.

Although these pressures affect all aspects of higher education, one could argue that student affairs is one of the areas that are particularly vulnerable. To illustrate this point, we re-visit the statement by Alan Guskin quoted in Chapter One:

> Strategically, enhancing student learning and reducing student costs are, in my judgment the primary yardstick [for organizational effectiveness]. Since the faculty and academic areas are most directly tied to student learning, alterations in the lower priority support areas must precede [major changes in the role of the faculty] (p. 29).

This assertion is one example of the consequences of focusing on student learning as the measure of institutional productivity: the aspects of the university that are most clearly associated with student learning have priority for funding, and, indeed, for surviving reductions in funding and personnel (Guskin, 1994a, 1994b). In such a climate, we should *expect* to hear the question, "Are student services and student affairs staff really necessary"? Because "most institutions lack evidence of the impact of out-of-class experiences on the learning and personal development of their students, yet many student affairs professionals and faculty steadfastly refuse to pick up the assessment tools that can remedy this situation" (Kuh, 1998, p. 21), student affairs can, indeed, be viewed as "a lower priority support area."

With assessment, student affairs organizations have the tools to find out — and show — the extent to which their programs, services, and people are, in fact, an integral aspect of student learning. Without assessment, "student affairs is left only to logic, intuition, moral imperatives, good will, or serendipity in justifying its existence." (Upcraft & Schuh, 1996, p. 12) In short, assessment can be a very important way of making the connection between what we do and the outcomes most valued by the institution.

There are, however, other reasons that student affairs professionals should have a strong commitment to assessment (Upcraft & Schuh, 1996). Even if the basic question of the value of student affairs to the institution has been answered in the affirmative, there are many other uses of assessment. Assessment can provide important information to deal with issues such as quality improvement and affordability and cost effectiveness. Assessment can also be important in strategic planning, policy development and decision making, and dealing with various political constituencies within and outside the institution.

For all these reasons, assessment is no longer "nice if you can afford it." Rather, you had better do it if you want to survive and improve. The *SLI* is an important first step in this transformation because it refocuses student affairs work at the core of the higher education enterprise *and* implies a set of measurable objectives, in the form of characteristics of learning-oriented student affairs divisions, that can provide the basis for an assessment agenda and plan.

SOME BASIC DEFINITIONS

One of the causes of confusion about assessment is terminology. Although there are many definitions of assessment, for the purposes of this chapter, we use Upcraft and Schuh's (1996) definition: "Assessment is any effort to gather, analyze, and interpret evidence which describes institutional, departmental, divisional, or agency effectiveness" (p.18). Upcraft and Schuh (1996) also argued that assessment must be contrasted with, though linked to, evaluation, which they define as "any effort to use assessment evidence to improve institutional, departmental, divisional, or agency effectiveness" (p.19). Put another way, whereas assessment describes effectiveness, evaluation is the application of assessment evidence to improve effectiveness, however that might be defined by an institution, department, division or agency.

Another term which muddies these definitional waters is "research." When comparing research and assessment, Erwin (1991) argued that although they share many processes in common, they differ in at least two respects. First, assessment guides good practice, while research guides theory and conceptual foundations. Second, assessment typically has implications for a single institution, but research typically has broader implications for student affairs work and higher education in general.

Given these definitions, this chapter is primarily about assessment. Some of what we address, however, could have implications for evaluation and research.

ASSESSING STUDENT LEARNING IN STUDENT AFFAIRS

We now return to the question posed at the beginning of this chapter: "What impact, if any, does student affairs have on student learning, and how do we know?" Our focus here is the assessment process in general — on how and where you can begin, or proceed more effectively, to answer that question in your own institution. Because of the very general nature of our discussion here, we suggest that the next step for anyone interested in planning for, and conducting, assessments in student affairs is to consult any or all of the excellent written resources on the topic. Several recent books offer detailed and thorough descriptions of techniques and approaches to assessing student learning outcomes, including outside the classroom (e.g., Angelo & Cross, 1993; Banta & Associates, 1993; Banta, et al., 1996; Kuh, et al., 1991; Stage,1992; Upcraft & Schuh, 1996). Useful frameworks and descriptions of student affairs research units, as well as possible agendas for assessment, also are available (e.g., Beeler & Hunter, 1991; Brown, 1991; Kuh, et al., 1991; Kuh, et al., 1994; Malaney, 1993; Malaney & Weitzer, 1993; Pascarella & Terenzini, 1998; Weitzer & Malaney, 1991). Instruments for studying students and their learning outside the classroom include the College Student Experience Questionnaire (e.g., Kuh, et al., 1994), the Community College Student Experience Questionnaire (e.g., Friedlander, Murrell, & MacDougall, 1993), and the Involving College Audit Protocol (Kuh, et al., 1991).

Issues to Consider

Developing and implementing effective assessments are complicated matters. But the experiences of people who have conducted them can provide a great deal of assistance and reassurance. For example, in their 1996 book, *Assessment in Student Affairs*, Upcraft and Schuh provided a summary of the "Principles of Good Practice for Assessment" (AAHE, 1992) as they might be applied to student affairs contexts. Although space concerns preclude detailed explanations of those principles here, we offer a brief description as a framework for getting started on an assessment plan.

1. Effective assessment of student affairs starts with educational values. Every assessment has a clearly-defined and well-understood purpose, and effective assessments are guided by the institution's mission and key values about students, their learning, and student affairs work and roles.

2. Effective assessments of student affairs understand "organizational outcomes as multidimensional, integrated, and revealed in performance over time" (Upcraft & Schuh, 1996, p. 22). Assessments should be as diverse and complex as the processes they seek to understand.
3. Effective student affairs assessments have clear and explicit goals.
4. Effective student affairs assessments are concerned with both outcomes and processes. What, for example, are the experiences and environments that contribute to learning outcomes?
5. Effective student affairs assessments are conducted over time, not just once.
6. Effective assessments in student affairs are the result of collaboration, within student affairs and with other campus groups — including students.
7. Effective student affairs assessments consider issues and questions that really matter. "This implies assessment approaches that produce evidence that the relevant parties will find credible, suggestive, and applicable to the decisions they must make" (Upcraft & Schuh, 1996, p. 24).

We would add, as well, that effective assessments begin with answers to the following questions: Why is the assessment being conducted? What is to be assessed and how? Who will be involved in the assessment, and in what ways? How will the results be analyzed and interpreted? With whom will the results be shared, and how will the results be used? (Upcraft & Schuh, 1996). Clear, shared understandings about the reasons for the assessment, the foci of the assessment, and the uses that will be made of assessment data are necessary in order to ensure that the assessment is not only useful, but ethical.

EXAMPLE OF AN OUTCOMES ASSESSMENT

Astin's (1991) input-environment-outcome (I-E-O) framework provides a well-researched and credible design for assessing learning.

> The primary purpose of Astin's I-E-O model is to identify and estimate institutional effects on how students grow or change during the

college years. In particular, this model is a useful tool for identifying and estimating effects of those college experiences over which institutions have some programmatic or policy control, such as student experiences, which can be shaped to educational advantage through an institution's programmatic or policy action, both inside and outside the classroom (Terenzini & Upcraft, 1996b, p. 219).

Astin's model posits that all educational outcomes are the result of a wide variety of personal, background, and educational characteristics students bring to college (inputs) acting in combination with the wide variety of experiences students have once they enroll (environment). Only when both inputs and experiences are taken into account can outcomes be accurately identified and understood. For example, determinations of change in students' attitudes toward diversity during college can be made only by taking into account the attitudes and characteristics of the students when they began (Pascarella, Edison, Nora, Hagedorn, & Terenzini, 1996).

In the remainder of this section we suggest how Astin's (1991) input-environment-outcome (IEO) framework might be used to assess the influence of a student affairs intervention. Perhaps the easiest and clearest way to accomplish this is by illustrating its application with an actual data-based example. The example we employ was part of an assessment carried out at Syracuse University to examine the educational effects of a residential intervention designed and administered by the Office of the Vice Chancellor for Student Affairs. [Published descriptions of this assessment and its findings are available in Kuh, Douglas, Lund & Ramin- Gyurnek (1994) and Pascarella & Terenzini (1980, 1991).] The university was concerned with improving the intellectual and cultural quality of student residential life during the first year of college. Based in part on some of the existing evidence on college impacts, it was hypothesized that one way to do this was by increasing the active role and influence of the institution's faculty in student residential life. To this end an experimental living-learning residence (hereafter referred to as the LLR) was designed to create a residence hall environment well integrated with the academic life of the university and in which active interchange among motivated students and faculty is promoted.

In addition to a number of other structural and programmatic features the LLR included seven live-in academic staff members; a faculty lecture series on current topics; an extensive series of credit and noncredit courses taught in the LLR; and a series of regularly scheduled informal discussions with faculty, deans, university administrators, and visiting scholars. It was anticipated that the LLR intervention would foster the growth of a distinctive set of influential interpersonal relationships, primarily between students and faculty, but also between and among students living in the LLR. Thus, the LLR was expected to influence major dimensions of the student's interpersonal and intellectual environment. In turn, it was hypothesized that the distinctive interpersonal and intellectual environment created by the LLR would foster, not only increased levels of student intellectual and personal development, but also on increased likelihood that students would persist from the first to the second year of college.

To ensure the internal validity of our assessment, we would have preferred, of course, to randomly assign students to the LLR intervention and to conventional or control residence halls. [By internal validity we mean the extent to which we can attribute the outcomes we observe to the intervention and not some competing cause or causes (Pascarella & Terenzini, 1991).] However, both the Vice Chancellor for Student Affairs and the institution's central administration felt that such a policy was untenable. Consequently assignment to the LLR or conventional residences was completely voluntary. This made our assessment more complex, but in all probability it more closely mirrored the reality of doing assessments in student affairs. Naturally occurring control groups are much more likely than the ability to conduct a true, randomized social experiment.

The self-selection of students into the LLR intervention and the conventional residences meant that the assessment had to collect extensive data on the same students over time and to rely on statistical procedures, such as multiple regression, to partial out or control the influences of potential confounding variables. It was in modeling the longitudinal nature of our assessment that Astin's (input-environment-output) was particularly useful. The IEO framework assumes that students come to an institution with a constellation of different intellectual and personal characteristics and proclivities. These precollege differences lead them to become differentially involved in different experiences during college (e.g., major, classwork, extracurricular activities, residence life, leisure time), which, in turn, shapes the extent to which they are influenced by the experience of college. Thus, there are two essential elements or characteristics of the IEO framework. First, it is longitudinal in nature. That is, it follows the same students over time. Second, it requires assessment of student precollege characteristics (inputs), assessment of different dimensions of the college experience (environments), and assessment of outcomes (outcomes).

Variables in the Assessment

Following the IEO framework, we collected three kinds of data on the students living in the LLR and conventional residences. First, a precollege questionnaire instrument was employed to collect students' expectations of college, background or demographic characteristics, and educational aspirations. In addition, verbal and quantitative scores on the SAT and rank in high school class were acquired from official university records. In all a battery of 15 student precollege characteristics were collected. Included were such variables as: educational aspirations and importance of graduating from college, academic aptitude and secondary school performance, family socioeconomic status, race, gender, and expectations of college in terms of involvement and satisfaction

The second set of variables collected constituted an attempt to measure dimensions of the students' interpersonal environment during the first year of college. These were defined operationally as whether the student lived in the LLR or conventional residence, and his or her responses to two scales measuring the quality and impact of interactions with faculty and a single scale measuring the quality and impact of interactions with peers. The three measures of interaction with faculty and peers were taken from Pascarella and Terenzini's (1980, 1983) institutional integration scales. These scales were labeled: (1) interactions with faculty (e.g. "my non-classroom interactions with faculty have had a positive influence on my personal growth, values and attitudes," "my non-classroom interactions with faculty have had a positive influence on my intellectual growth and interest in ideas."); (2) faculty concern for student development and teaching (e.g., "few of the faculty members I have had contact with are generally interested in students," "few of the faculty members I have had contact with are willing to spend time outside class to discuss issues of interest and importance to students"- items coded in reverse); and (3) peer-group interactions (e.g., "my interpersonal relationships with other students have had a positive influence on my personal growth, attitudes, and values," "my interpersonal relationships with other students have had a positive influence on my intellectual growth and interest in ideas"). These data were collected on a follow-up questionnaire administered near the end of the first year of college.

The final set of variables we collected was measures of three outcomes hypothesized to be influenced by the LLR intervention. These were operationalized as self-reported gains in personal and intellectual development, and persistence from the first to the second year of college. The personal development scale asked students to indicate their progress (1= no progress to 4= a great deal of progress) in seven areas (e.g., "clearer/better understanding of myself," "developing interpersonal skills"). The intellectual development scale asked students to indicate their progress in four areas, (e.g., applying abstractions and principles in problem solving," "critical evaluation of ideas"). Information on the personal and intellectual development scales was collected on the follow-up questionnaire. The persistence variable was operationally defined as those students in the sample who reenrolled for their second year at the institution versus those who withdrew voluntarily and did not reenroll.

Data Analysis in the Assessment

Step 1: Verification of the Intervention. We made a small modification of the IEO framework in our data analysis, though it is one we believe is essential to better understanding the impact of student affairs interventions. Since one purpose of the LLR was to create a distinctive set of influential relationships with faculty and peers our first analytical step was to ascertain whether or not that in fact happened. In short, we sought to verify the intervention by estimating the impact of the LLR (versus conventional residences) on the interactions with faculty, the faculty concern for student development and teaching, and the peer-group interactions scales. Figure 1 shows how we conceptualized our analysis to verify the intervention. As the figure suggests we assumed that each of the interpersonal environment scales would be a function of student background characteristics and whether they lived in the LLR or conventional residences. Consequently, we performed three regression analyses in which each of the interpersonal environment scales was regressed on (or predicted with) the 15 student background characteristics plus a categorical variable indicating if the student lived in the LLR (coded 1) or the conventional residences (coded 0).

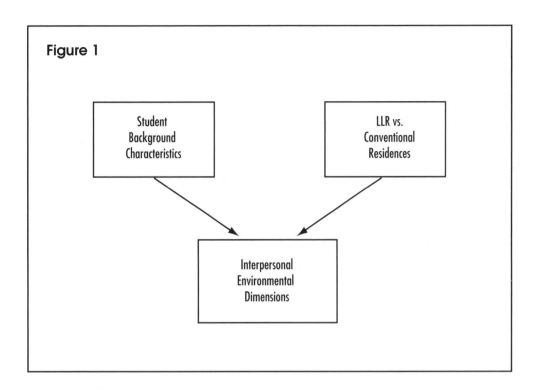

Figure 1

The results of this first step in our analyses indicated that, in the presence of statistical controls for student background characteristics, living in the LLR (versus conventional residences) was positively and significantly associated with each of the three interpersonal environment scales. In other words, even with student background characteristics controlled statistically, students in the LLR had significantly higher scores than their counterparts in conventional residence halls on the interactions with faculty scale, the faculty concern for student development and teaching scale, and the peer-group interactions scale. Thus, there was evidence to suggest the LLR was in fact creating a distinctive interpersonal environment in terms of students' interactions with faculty and peers.

Step 2: Does the Intervention Influence the Outcomes? In this stage of the assessment we sought to determine if the intervention variable (LLR=1, Conventional Residences=0) is associated with the anticipated outcomes: progress in intellectual and personal development and first-year persistence/withdrawal behavior. Figure 2

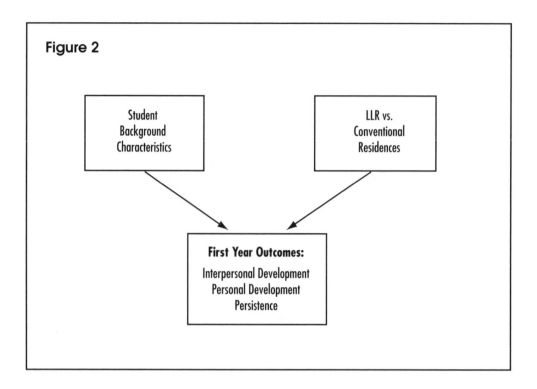

Figure 2

shows how we conceptualized this part of the assessment. As the Figure indicates we assumed that each of the three outcome measures would be a function of student background characteristics and whether they lived in the LLR or conventional residences. Thus, we performed three additional regression analyses in which each of the three outcomes was regressed on (or predicted by) the 15 student background characteristics plus the categorical variable indicating if the student lived in the LLR or the conventional residences.

With differences in students' background characteristics held constant statistically the LLR students as a group were found to report significantly greater progress on the intellectual and personal development scales, and to have a significantly higher rate of first-to second-year persistence than students in the conventional residences. Although this was welcome news it suggested only that the overall environment of the LLR had a positive influence on each of the outcomes. It does not suggest which particular dimension of the LLR accounted for this overall influence. To shed light on the latter issue we extended the assessment to a third step.

Step 3: Do the Verified Dimensions of the Intervention Account for Its Effects on the Outcomes? In the first two steps of our assessment we found evidence to suggest: (1) the LLR intervention did foster a distinctive set of interpersonal relationships between students and faculty and between students and their peers, and (2) the LLR had a positive influence on students' end-of-first-year intellectual and personal development, as well as their persistence from the first to the second year of college. In the final stage of the assessment we try to better understand *why* the LLR had the impact that it did on the outcome measures. To accomplish this we estimate the extent to which the distinctive interpersonal dimensions of the LLR account for its impact on the outcome measures. Figure 3 illustrates how we conceptualize this final step in the assessment. As the Figure suggests we assumed that each of the outcome measures would be a function of 1) student background characteristics; 2) whether the student lived in the LLR (versus conventional residences); and 3) the three interpersonal environment dimensions fostered by the LLR. However, we also anticipated that the influence of the LLR on each of the outcomes would be accounted for (or mediated

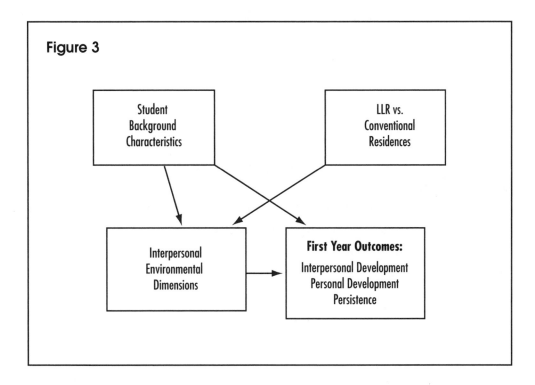

Figure 3

by) the distinctive interpersonal environment fostered by the LLR. Thus, we expected that the effect of the categorical variable representing participation in the LLR versus conventional residences would become small and non-significant when the effects of the interactions with faculty scale, the faculty concern for student development and teaching scale, and the peer-group interactions scale were also taken into account. In short we expected that the composite effects of the LLR on the outcome measures would be accounted for, and mediated through, the distinctive interpersonal environment that it fosters.

We therefore carried out a final set of analyses in which each of the three outcomes measures (i.e., intellectual development, personal development and persistence) was regressed on (or predicted by) the battery of student precollege characteristics, the categorical variable indicating LLR or conventional residence, and the three interpersonal environment dimensions significantly influenced by the LLR (i.e., interactions with faculty, faculty concern for student development and teaching, and peer-group interactions). The results of these analyses generally supported expectations. Statistically controlling for student background characteristics, each of the three interpersonal environment dimensions had a significant positive association with each of the three outcome measures. The same, however, was not true of the categorical variable indicating LLR or conventional residence. When the interpersonal environment dimensions were added to the equation the effect of the categorical variable indicating residence option became small and non-significant. This suggests that the three interpersonal environment dimensions shown to be influenced by the LLR capture all the significant effects of the LLR on the three end-of-first-year outcomes. It is at this point that the assessment helps us understand just how exposure to the LLR exerted its influence on students' intellectual and personal development, and persistence. It appears to have done so by fostering a distinctive set of interpersonal relationships with faculty and peers. Had the effect of the categorical variable indicating residence option remained significant, it would have suggested that the three interpersonal environment dimension did not account for the total positive effects of the LLR on the outcomes.

RECOMMENDATIONS AND REFINEMENTS

We believe the modification of Astin's (1991) IEO framework introduced and illustrated above has several strengths in assessing the effects of any programmatic intervention in student affairs. First, by requiring that the underlying process dimensions of the intervention be specified and operationally defined, the framework forces the individual conducting the assessment to consider in some detail just why the intervention should have an influence on certain outcomes. Second, the framework requires the intervention to be empirically verified in terms of the particular social-psychological processes that it fosters, thereby permitting an assessment of the extent to which the intervention was implemented as intended. Finally the assessment procedures of the framework focus not merely on the gross effects of an intervention but, rather, on the extent to which the specific underlying process dimensions of the intervention account for its overall influence on the outcomes. Such evidence may be particularly useful in identifying those specific dimensions or components of an intervention that have the greatest impact on a desired outcome.

As with any assessment framework, the usefulness of the findings, in terms of policy implications, depends most heavily on the data employed and the care with which the assessment is conducted. Clearly considerable care and thought must attend the operational definition and measurement of the process dimensions of any student affairs intervention. Before substantial human and fiscal resources are invested in any large intervention designed to influence student development, however, it would be probably wise to first "pilot" the program on a small scale. This permits one to identify and work out the "bugs" that inevitably occur the first time any complex programmatic intervention is tried. The first step in our suggested assessment framework (verifying the intervention) can be quite useful at the pilot stage for identifying those components of the intervention that were implemented as planned and those that were not. It probably makes sense to worry about assessing the impact of an intervention on student outcomes only after there is some reasonable assurance that intervention is being implemented or carried out as planned.

Two additional points are worthy of mention. First, be sensitive to the indirect effects of programmatic interventions. The impact of student affairs interventions on a range of student outcomes may not always be straightforward or obvious. For example, a study by Pascarella, Terenzini and Wolfle (1986) indicated that the hypothesized direct effects of a comprehensive student orientation program on student persistence after the first year of college were small and non-significant. However, students attending orientation (versus those who did not) were more proficient in developing a set of coping skills that led to more successful integration into the academic and social systems of the institution. In turn, those students more successfully integrated into the institutions' academic and social systems were also more likely to persist at the institution from the first to the second year. Thus, the assessment indicated that, although student orientation had little or no direct influence on student persistence, it nevertheless had a rather substantial and significant, positive indirect effect on persistence. We would argue that unless such indirect effects are assessed it may be quite easy to underestimate or even dismiss the influence of many student affairs interventions on student development.

Second, be sensitive to the possibility that the effects of student affairs interventions are conditional rather than general. A general effect means that a certain experience has the same influence for all people exposed to it. A conditional effect means that the extent of the influence of a certain experience varies for different kinds of students. For example, recent research from the National Study of Student Learning found that fraternity membership had a substantial, negative effect on the first-year cognitive growth of white men. For men of color, however, the cognitive effect of fraternity membership was slightly positive (Pascarella, Edison, Whitt, Nora, Hagedorn, & Terenzini, 1996).

Because of the growing diversity of the postsecondary education student body, conditional effects are not only more important, they are also more likely to occur. There is an increased probability that the developmental impact of any programmatic intervention will vary in magnitude, and perhaps even in direction, for different kinds of students. Thus, assessments that consider only the general effects of an intervention may mask important variations in the size of those effects for important subgroups of students.

CONCLUSION

According to the *Student Learning Imperative* (ACPA, 1994), learning-oriented student affairs divisions are places where staff are experts on students and their learning, as well as the environments in which that learning takes place. Such expertise requires systematic inquiry, including assessments of the impact of student affairs programs and services (Whitt & Pascarella, 1999). In addition, in learning-oriented student affairs divisions, decisions about what to do and what not to do (e.g., what activities to engage in and what activities to stop or avoid (Kuh, 1998)) "are based on promising practices from the research on student learning and institution-specific assessment data" (ACPA, 1994, p. 4). External and internal pressures to demonstrate contributions to essential institutional goals as a means to ensure survival are important reasons for conducting assessments in student affairs. But the most important reasons are our students, and our commitment to them and their learning.

CHAPTER 6

Responding to Our Student Learning Imperative

Elizabeth J. Whitt

Like most professionals, I was taught to occupy space, not open it.
—Palmer, 1997, p. 9

We began this monograph with a set of questions: What does the student affairs "landscape" — both outside and inside our institutions — look like? What does "student learning" mean in the context of student affairs work? How does student affairs contribute to student learning outcomes, and how do we know? How do we go about creating and maintaining learning-oriented student affairs divisions? The preceding chapters addressed many aspects of these questions and offered what we hope are useful ideas and implications. But at this stage of the paradigm shift, *answers* are in short supply. As odd as it sounds, this can be viewed as good news. Reflecting on and redefining student affairs practice to meet our student learning imperative is a journey we have only begun. So questioning all aspects of our work and taking time to experiment with new mental models and new behaviors appropriate to the learning paradigm — while resisting the temptation to quickly substitute new certainties for old — is a healthy first step (Kuh, Whitt, & Shedd, 1987). To assist in embarking on this adventure, next we provide a few suggestions and many more questions to sustain you, and provoke your own learning, on your way.

The suggestions are organized according to the varying roles each student affairs professional is likely to play: member of the student affairs profession, university administrator, and educator in relationships with students. Although these roles are not carried out independent of one another, they can lead to different ways of thinking about, and promoting, student learning. In addition, context is important; the nature of the roles any of us plays varies, for example, by institution and by time in career, so such issues should be kept in mind as you think about how to use these suggestions. Following the action items we pose some of the questions we in the Student Learning Project Work Group have asked ourselves as we think about how our work and how our professional lives will be different when we put student learning at the center.

SUGGESTIONS FOR THE JOURNEY

Role: Student Affairs Professional

Implicit in the description of a professional are education, reflection, and a commitment to ongoing learning and development. And, in choosing to become student affairs professionals, we enter a broader community of learners — the community of learners involved in the higher education of students. It is essential, therefore, that we become active participants in that community, engaging student affairs colleagues on our campuses and through our professional associations to examine what we believe and what we think we know, and to ask why, how, what our students are learning. We offer the following suggestions and questions to facilitate our development as professionals in the context of our learning imperative:

▶ Recognize, understand, and challenge your assumptions — including assumptions about student affairs work, what matters in undergraduate education, what *others* think matters in undergraduate education, how to define student learning, students (and what they learn and how), and your contributions to student learning.

▶ Be a learner. What do you need to know and be able to do to foster your *own* learning? What do you need to know and be able to do to foster the learning of others?

▶ Ask questions — of yourself, your colleagues, your students — to reflect on what you are learning.

▶ Know how students learn — become an expert on learning, including research on student learning outside classrooms.

▶ Ask yourself:
What is my professional development plan — what do I want and
need to learn about this semester? This year? What do I know and
understand about how students learn? What do I know and use of
research on student learning in college? What assumptions do I make
about students — students in general, and the students with whom
I work in particular? When my assumptions are derived from my
relationships with students, what data have I gathered to confirm
my observations? What should I read? How will I make time to read?

Role: College or University Administrator

The role of a student affairs professional is integrated with that of university
administrator (broadly defined to include all "levels" of student affairs work). Central
to the role of administrator is commitment to the purposes of higher education and
the mission and purposes of our particular institutions. This commitment implies
an understanding of learning — the creation, dissemination, and application of
knowledge — as the core purpose and product of a university. Achieving such
understanding brings additional commitments, including engagement in the life of
the mind, however that is defined within a particular college or university. Examples
could include attending a university lecture and performing arts series, participating
in seminars on teaching and learning, and collaborating with academic colleagues to
seek answers to the questions we share. The specific actions are less important than
the general, lived commitment to learning as the essential activity of higher education
— and so, of student affairs professionals.

Being leaders and managers are different but related roles for student affairs
administrators. Leaders create visions; managers implement visions. It is critical that
we as administrators take the steps that permit us to place student learning at the
center of student affairs practice. For example, as administrators, we are responsible
for the planning and assessment processes which guide our policies and practices.
Good planning starts with a mission and defined learning outcomes. It comes full
circle when we complete outcomes assessment. Using an integrated planning and
assessment model provides a context for sound decision making on program planning
and resource allocation. Ultimately, we have the responsibility to question everything

we do AND we have to quit doing some things we have always done and love to do.

The following suggestions address challenges posed by the learning imperative for our role as administrators:

▶ Know and understand your institution's mission for learning, and how that mission is (and should be) implemented.

▶ Examine the mental models of learning found in your institution — faculty, student affairs, students, external stakeholders — and identify implications for fostering learning.

▶ Understand the multiple lenses used to define learning, as well as other desired outcomes of colleges.

▶ Work with student affairs and academic colleagues, students and others to develop a common view of learning.

▶ Find partners beyond your department and beyond student affairs to develop goals and plans for achieving the institution's mission for learning.

▶ Engage in activities which support the intellectual life of the institution, and the intellectual life of students.

▶ Become well-informed about the academic requirements of your institution, and the academic activities and responsibilities of the students with whom you work.

▶ Ask yourself:

What is my institution's mission? Why does the university need my department/my position to accomplish its mission? What is the student affairs division's mission for learning, and how is that mission implemented? What contributions do I (can I) make to the learning mission? With whom can I collaborate to assist students in making connections among all their learning experiences? How can I learn about the diversity of perspectives among our university community members? How can I become a role model for learning? How do I demonstrate my commitment to knowledge and "the life of the mind"?

As a manager, do I remember that good management is a tool to further opportunities for student learning? As a leader, do I keep students and their learning in the center of my communication about our purpose and our enterprise? Do staff with whom I work know and believe that student learning is our purpose? How do we create environments and experiences that promote learning? How do we create environments and experiences which are not barriers to learning?

Role: Educator in Relationships with Students

We should keep in mind our varied roles with students: teacher, coach, guide, mentor, advisor, role model, and caring professional. Some of what students need to learn is — or should be — found in their interactions with us and in their interactions with others (students, faculty) in the environments we help to create. We know that students learn more and more effectively if their interactions with others reinforce institutional goals for learning (Kuh et al., 1994; Terenzini et al., 1996; Whitt et al., 1999a). Students also benefit from — and need help making —connections between what they learn in different settings – a history class and an English class, a political science class and student government, job and the career position to which he or she aspires. Finally, students need our help in making meaning of their experiences. We often do our most effective "teaching" through asking questions and challenging students to find their own answers by making connections among the learning they do in all of their collegiate experiences.

A critical issue to be addressed by student affairs professionals is the extent to which activities with which we have traditionally engaged with students do, in fact, foster learning. And which activities students can, and will, provide for themselves so that scarce staff time can be used to enhance student learning. Some have asked how one might, for example, identify and foster the learning outcomes of rock concerts, picnics, or sports events— other than for the students who are involved in planning and implementing those events, or as needed for risk management. Perhaps a more useful question, in a time of doing more with less — or even less with less (Levine, 1997) — is whether staff time is best used helping students entertain themselves.

We offer the following to help student affairs professionals in educational roles with students:

▶ Expect students to be involved in their learning and help them take responsibility for that learning.

▶ Explain to students what they are expected to learn — and maintain high, clear, expectations for learning.

▶ Ask students about their learning.

▶ Ask students to make meaning from their learning; ask them to connect current learning to other current learning and current learning to their future.

▶ Ask yourself:

Do I communicate to students how important their learning is to me? Do I ask students what they have learned? Do I ask them to apply what they have learned through our shared experience to what they have learned in classes? [and vice versa] Do I know and think about how students learn? Do I consider the differences in learning styles and mastery of content when planning educational experiences for students? When serving as an adviser, do I think about how I can foster learning? Do I ask what students can learn and should learn from each contact I have with students? How do I know that learning has occurred? How do students demonstrate their progress and mastery? How can I systematically collect data about student learning?

CONCLUSION

The student affairs "landscape" of the late 1990s presents many challenges, including unprecedented change, shrinking resources, and declining public confidence. These challenges — and others — are complex and difficult to address, and so they seem, at times, insurmountable obstacles to accomplishing our tasks. Yet the "new dawn" of higher education also provides an opportunity to look at our landscape with a fresh perspective, informed by an exciting shift in focus in higher education to students and their learning. This shift, too, is good news for student affairs professionals. If, in our colleges and universities, "all serve learning" (NASULGC, 1997, p.17) and if the purpose of our institutions is to create powerful learning environments and opportunities for students, then student affairs work is at the heart of our institutions.

Shifting paradigms, even in directions that are good for us, can, however, be frightening (Barr & Tagg, 1995; Kuh, Whitt, & Shedd, 1987). There is comfort in old ways and security in old perspectives, especially in times of great stress. But there is also a great deal of evidence that the challenges we face now will not go away and that we retreat to familiar activities and ideas at our peril. Just as Dr. Martin Luther King, Jr. admonished his colleagues that the civil rights movement faced the alternatives of "chaos or community," so the university presidents who composed the NASULGC report (1997) stated in no uncertain terms that "unless we become the architects of change, we will become its victims" (p. 9). The choice posed here applies not only to university presidents, but to all of us who work in higher education.

The fact that our profession has its own *Student Learning Imperative* (ACPA, 1994) also is good news. The *SLI* provides a map for exploring the landscape of the Learning Paradigm and a framework for assessing the effectiveness of our current methods and assumptions and beliefs in this new territory. It challenges us, for example, to recognize that our programs, activities, and services are *means*, not ends — that is, *means* to develop learning opportunities rather than ends in themselves (Kuh, 1996b). Perhaps most important, the *SLI* reminds us that "student affairs must model what we wish for our students: an ever-increasing capacity for learning and self-reflection."

Allen, K.E., and Garb, E.L. (1993). Reinventing student affairs: Something old and something new. *NASPA Journal, 30(2)*, 93-100.

American Association for Higher Education (1992). *Principles of good practice for assessing student learning.* Washington, DC: Author.

American College Personnel Association (1994). *The student learning imperative: Implications for student affairs.* Washington, DC: Author.

American College Personnel Association and National Association of Student Personnel Administrators (1998). *Principles of good practice for student affairs.* Washington, DC: Author.

American College Testing Program (1991). *CAAP technical handbook.* Iowa City, IA: Author.

Arnold, K.D. (1995). *Lives of Promise: What becomes of high school valedictorians.* San Francisco: Jossey-Bass.

Astin, A. (1984). Student involvement: A developmental theory for higher education. *Journal of College Student Personnel, 25,* 297-308.

Astin, A. (1991). *Assessment for excellence: The philosophy and practice of assessment and evaluation in higher education.* New York: ACE-Macmillan.

Astin, A. (1993). *What matters in college: Four critical years revisited.* San Francisco: Jossey-Bass.

Astin, A. (1996). *Involvement in Learning* revisited: Lessons we have learned. *Journal of College Student Development, 37,* 123-133.

Astin, A. (1998). The changing American college student: Thirty-year trends, 1966-1996. *Review of Higher Education, 21,* 115-136.

Attinasi, L.C., Jr. (1989). Getting in: Mexican Americans' perceptions of university attendance and the implications for freshman year persistence. *Journal of Higher Education, 60,* 247-277.

Atwell, R.H. (1994). Higher education and the path to progress. In D.H. Finifter & A.M. Hauptman (Eds.), America's investment in liberal education (pp. 125-132). *New Directions For Higher Education, No. 85.* San Francisco: Jossey-Bass.

Ballou, R. (1997). Reorganizing student affairs for the twenty-first century. *About Campus, 2*(5), 24-25.

Banta, T.W. and Associates (1995). *Making a difference: Outcomes of a decade of assessment in higher education.* San Francisco: Jossey-Bass.

Banta, T.W., Lund, J.P., Black, K.E., & Oblander, F.W. (1996). *Assessment in practice: Putting principles to work on college campuses.* San Francisco: Jossey-Bass.

Barr, R.B., & Tagg, J. (1995). From teaching to learning: A new paradigm for undergraduate education. *Change, 27*(6), 12-25.

Baxter Magolda, M.B. (1992). *Knowing and reasoning in college: Gender-related patterns in students' intellectual development.* San Francisco: Jossey-Bass.

Baxter Magolda, M.B. (1995). The integration of relational and impersonal knowing in young adults' epistemological development. *Journal of College Student Development, 36,* 205-216.

Baxter Magolda, M.B. (1996). Cognitive learning and personal development: A false dichotomy. *About Campus, 1*(3), 16-21.

Beeler, K.J., & Hunter, D.E. (1991). The promise of student affairs research. In K.J. Beeler & D.E. Hunter (Eds.), *Puzzles and pieces in wonderland: The promise and practice of student affairs research* (pp. 1-17). Washington, DC: National Association of Student Personnel Administrators.

Belenky, M., Clinchy, B., Goldberger, N., & Tarule, J. (1986). *Women's ways of knowing: The development of self, voice, and mind.* New York: Basic Books.

Berger, J.B. (1997). Students' sense of community in residence halls, social integration, and first-year persistence. *Journal of College Student Development, 38,* 441-452.

Blake, E.S. (1979). Classroom and context: An educational dialect. *Academe, 65,* 280-292.

Blake, E.S. (1996). The yin and yang of student learning in college. *About Campus, 1*(4), 4-9.

Blimling, G.S. (1993). The influence of college residence halls on students. In J.S. Smart (Ed.), *Higher education: Handbook of theory and research* (Vol. 9) (pp. 248-307).

Blimling, G.S., & Alschuler, A.S. (1996). Creating a home for the spirit of learning: Contributions of student development educators. *Journal of College Student Development, 37,* 203-316.

Blimling, G.S., & Whitt, E.J. (1998). Creating and using principles of good practice for student affairs. *About Campus, 3*(1), 10-15.

Bloland, P.A., Stamatakos, L.C., & Rogers, R. R. (1994). *Reform in student affairs: A critique of student development.* Greensboro, NC: ERIC Counseling and Student Services Clearinghouse.

Bloland, P.A., Stamatakos, L.C., & Rogers, R. R. (1996). Redirecting the role of student affairs to focus on student learning. *Journal of College Student Development, 37,* 217-226.

Boyer Commission on Educating Undergraduates in the Research University (1998). *Reinventing undergraduate education: A blueprint for America's research universities.* Stony Brook, NY: State University of New York.

Brown, J.S. (1997). On becoming a learning organization. *About Campus, 1(6),* 5-10.

Brown, R.D. (1972). *Student development in tomorrow's higher education: A return to the academy* [Student Personnel Series No. 16]. Washington, DC: American College Personnel Association.

Brown, R.D. (1991). Student affairs research on trial. In K.J. Beeler & D.E. Hunter (Eds.), *Puzzles and Pieces in Wonderland: The Promise and Practice of Student Affairs Research* (pp. 124-142). Washington, DC: National Association of Student Personnel Administrators.

Brown, R.D. (1996). We've been there. We've done that. Let's keep it up. *Journal of College Student Development, 37,* 239-241.

Bruffee, K.A. (1995). Intention "misunderstood." *Change, 27(5),* 6,62.

Caple, R.B. (1996). The learning debate: A historical perspective. *Journal of College Student Development, 37,* 193-203.

Chickering, A.W. (1981). *The modern American college.* San Francisco: Jossey-Bass.

Chickering A.W., & Reisser, L. (1993). *Education and identity.* (2nd ed.) San Francisco: Jossey-Bass.

Cross, K.P. (1996). New lenses on learning. *About Campus, 1(1),* 4-9.

Erlich, T. (1991). *Our university in the state: Educating the new majority.* Bloomington, IN: Indiana University.

Erwin, T.D. (1996). Assessment, evaluation, and research. In S.R. Komives, D.B. Woodard, & Associates, *Student Services: A Handbook for the Profession* (pp. 415-434). 3rd. ed. San Francisco: Jossey-Bass.

Evanoski, P. (1988). An assessment of the impact of helping on the helper for college students. *College Student Journal, 22(1)*, 2-6.

Fenske, R.H. (1989). Historical foundations of student services. In U. Delworth, G. Hanson, & Associates (Eds.), *Student services: A handbook for the profession* (2nd ed.) (pp. 5-24) San Francisco: Jossey-Bass.

Fuller, B.E., & Hall, F.J. (1996). Differences in personality type and roommate compatibility as predictors of roommate conflict. *Journal of College Student Development, 37*, 510-518.

Goleman, D. (1995). *Emotional intelligence*. New York: Bantam.

Goodman, H. (1995, September 25). College debts have families "at crossroads". *The Philadelphia Enquirer* A1, 13.

Guskin, A.E. (1994a). Reducing student costs and enhancing student learning, part I: Restructuring the administration. *Change, 26(4)*, 22-29.

Guskin, A.E. (1994b). Reducing student costs and enhancing student learning, part II: Restructuring the role of faculty. *Change, 26(5)*, 16-25.

Guskin, A.E. (1997). Learning more, spending less. *About Campus, 2(3)*, 4-9

Hanson, G. (1991). The call to assessment: What role for student affairs? In K.J. Beeler & D.E. Hunter (Eds.), *Puzzles and pieces in wonderland: The promise and practice of student affairs research* (pp. 80-105). Washington, DC: National Association of Student Personnel Administrators.

Hitchings, W.E., Luzzo, D.A., Retish, P., Horvath, M., & Ristow, R.S. (1998). Identifying the career development needs of college students with disabilities. *Journal of College Student Development, 39*, 23-32.

Horowitz, H.L. (1987). *Campus life: Undergraduate cultures from the end of the eighteenth century to the present.* New York: Knopf.

Hutchings, P. (1996). Building a new culture of teaching and learning. *About Campus, 1*(5), 4-8.

Inman, P., & Pascarella, E.T. (in press). The impact of college residence on the development of critical thinking in college freshmen. *Journal of College Student Development.*

Jacoby, B. (1989). *The student as commuter: Developing a comprehensive institutional response. ASHE-ERIC Higher Education Report no. 7.* Washington, DC: School of Education and Human Development, The George Washington University.

Jones, S.R. (1997). Voices of identity and difference: A qualitative exploration of the multiple dimensions of identity development in women college students. *Journal of College Student Development, 38,* 376-386.

Kalsbeek, D.H. (1994). New perspectives for assessing the residential experience. In C. Schroeder & P. Mable (Eds.), *Realizing the educational potential of residence halls* (pp. 269-297). San Francisco: Jossey-Bass.

Katchadourian, H. & Boli, J. (1994). *Cream of the crop: The impact of elite education in the decade after college.* New York: Basic Books.

Kauffman, N., & Kuh, G.D. (1985). The impact of study abroad on personal development of college students. *Journal of International Student Personnel, 2*(2), 6-10.

Kegan, R. (1994). *In over our heads: The mental demands of modern life.* Cambridge, MA: Harvard University Press.

Kerr, C. (1994). *Troubled times for American higher education.* Albany, NY: State University of New York Press.

King, M.L. Jr. (1967). Where do we go from here: Chaos or community? In J.M. Washington (1986). (Ed.), *A testament of hope: The essential writings and speeches of Martin Luther King, Jr.* (pp. 555-575). San Francisco: Harpers..

King, P.M. (1996). Student cognition and learning. In S. R. Komives and D. B. Woodard (Eds.), *Student services: A handbook for the profession.* (3rd ed.) (pp. 218-243). San Francisco: Jossey-Bass.

King, P.M., & Baxter Magolda, M.B. (1996). A developmental perspective on learning. *Journal of College Student Development, 37,*163-172.

Kluge, P.F. (1993). *Alma mater: A college homecoming.* Reading, MA: Addison-Wesley.

Kuh, G.D. (1993). In their own words: What students learn outside the classroom. *American Educational Research Journal, 30,* 277-304.

Kuh, G.D. (1994, September) *The student learning imperative? What is it? Why now? What does it mean?* Keynote address, National Symposium on Student Learning and Gerald Saddlemire Memorial Lecture, Bowling Green, Ohio.

Kuh, G.D. (1995). The other curriculum: Out-of-class experiences associated with student learning and personal development. *Journal of Higher Education, 66,* 123-155.

Kuh, G.D. (1996a). Guiding principles for creating seamless learning environments for undergraduates. *Journal of College Student Development, 37,* 135-148.

Kuh, G.D. (1996b). Some things we should forget. *About Campus, 1(4),* 10-15.

Kuh, G.D. (1997). You gotta believe! *About Campus, 2(4),* 2-3.

Kuh, G.D. (1998). Lessons from the mountains. *About Campus, 3(2),* 16-21.

Kuh, G.D., Branch Douglas, K., Lund, J.P., & Ramin-Gyurnek, J. (1994). *Student learning outside the classroom: Transcending artificial boundaries.* ASHE-ERIC Higher Education Report, No. 8. Washington, DC: The George Washington University.

Kuh, G.D., & Lund, J.P. (1994). What students gain from participating in student government. In M. Terrell & M. Cuyjet (Eds.), Developing student government leadership. *New Directions for Student Services* (No. 66). San Francisco: Jossey-Bass.

Kuh, G.D., Pace, C.R., & Vesper, N. (1997). The development of process indicators to estimate student gains associated with good practices in undergraduate education. *Research in Higher Education, 38*, 435-454.

Kuh, G.D., Schuh, J.H., Whitt, E.J. & Associates. (1991). *Involving colleges: Successful approaches to fostering student learning and development outside the classroom.* San Francisco: Jossey-Bass.

Kuh, G.D., Vesper, N., & Krehbiel, L. (1994). Student learning at metropolitan universities. J. Smart (Ed.), *Higher Education: Handbook of theory and research,* Vol. 10 (1-44). New York: Agathon.

Kuh, G.D., & Whitt, E.J. (1988). *The invisible tapestry: Cultures of American colleges and universities.* ASHE-ERIC Higher Education Report, No. 1. Washington, DC: Association for the Study of Higher Education.

Kuh, G.D., Whitt, E.J., & Shedd, J.D. (1987). *Student affairs work, 2001: A paradigmatic odyssey.* Alexandria, VA: ACPA Media.

Levine, A. (1997). Higher education becomes a mature industry. *About Campus, 2*(3), 31-32.

Levine, A., & Cureton, J.S. (1998a). Collegiate life: An obituary. *Change, 30*(3), 12-17, 51.

Levine, A., & Cureton, J.S. (1998b). *When hope and fear collide*. San Francisco: Jossey-Bass.

London, H. B. (1996). How college affects first-generation students. *About Campus, 1*(5), 9-13.

Loevinger, J. (1976). *Ego development: Conceptions and theories*. San Francisco: Jossey-Bass.

Luzzo, D.A., McWhirter, E.H., & Hutcheson, K.G. (1997). Evaluating career decision-making factors associated with employment among first-year college students. *Journal of College Student Development, 38*, 166-172.

Magolda, P. M. (1997). Life as I don't know it. *About Campus, 2*(2), 16-22.

Malaney, G.D. (1993). A comprehensive student affairs research office. *NASPA Journal, 30*, 182-89.

Malaney, G.D., & Weitzer, W.H. (1993). Research on students: A framework of methods based on cost and expertise. *NASPA Journal, 30*, 126-137.

Marchese, T. (1994, March). *Assessment*. Paper presented at the annual meeting of the American College Personnel Association, Indianapolis, IN.

Mather, P.C., & Winston, R.B. (1998). Autonomy development of traditional-aged students: Themes and processes. *Journal of College Student Development, 39*, 33-50.

Matthews, A. (1997). *Bright college years*. New York: Simon and Schuster.

Moffatt, M. (1989). *Coming of age in New Jersey: College and American culture*. New Brunswick, NJ: Rutgers University Press.

National Association of State Universities and Land Grant Colleges (1997). Returning to our roots: The student experience. Washington, DC: Author.

National Association of Student Personnel Administrators (1989). *Points of view.* Washington, DC: Author.

National Association of Student Personnel Administrators (1995, November). *NASPA strategic plan.* Washington, DC: Author.

National Association of Student Personnel Administrators (1996). *Monograph preview.* Washington, DC: Author.

National Center for Education Statistics (1994). *The condition of education.* Washington, DC: United States Department of Education.

Newton, F.B. (1998). The stressed student — How can we help? *About Campus, 3(2),* 4-10.

Noddings, N. (1991). Stories in dialogue: Caring and interpersonal reasoning. In C. Witherell & N. Noddings (Eds.), *Stories lives tell: Narrative and dialogue in education.* (pp. 157-170). New York: Teachers College Press.

Pace, C.R. & Baird, L.L. (!966). Attainment patterns in the environmental press of college subcultures. In T. Newcomb and E. Wilson (Eds.), *College peer groups* (pp. 215-242). Chicago: Aldine.

Pace, C.R. (1990). *The undergraduates: A report of their activities and progress in college in the 1980s.* Los Angeles: Center for the Study of Evaluation, UCLA Graduate School of Education.

Palmer, P. (1990). Good teaching: A matter of living the mystery. *Change,* 11-16.

Palmer, P. (1997). Teaching and learning in community. *About Campus, 2(5),* 4-13.

Pascarella, E.T. (1991). The impact of college on students: The nature of the evidence. *Review of Higher Education, 14,* 453-466.

Pascarella, E.T. (1995). The impact of college on students: Myths, rational myths, and some other things that may not be true. *NACADA Journal, 15(2),* 26-33.

Pascarella, E.T. (1997a). College's influence on principled moral reasoning. *Educational Record, 78* (3,4), 47-55.

Pascarella, E.T. (1997b). It's time we started paying attention to community college students. *About Campus, 1(6),* 14-17.

Pascarella, E.T., Bohr, L., Nora, A., Zusman, B., Inman, P., & Desler, M. (1993). Cognitive impacts of living on campus versus commuting to college. *Journal of College Student Development, 34,* 216-220.

Pascarella, E.T., Edison, M.I., Nora, A., Hagedorn, L.S., & Terenzini, P.T. (1998a). Does community college versus four-year college attendance influence students' educational plans? *Journal of College Student Development, 39,* 179-193.

Pascarella, E.T., Edison, M.I., Nora, A., Hagedorn, L.S., & Terenzini, P.T. (1998b). Does work inhibit cognitive development during college? *Educational Evaluation and Policy Analysis, 20,* 75-93.

Pascarella, E.T., Edison, M., Nora, A., Hagedorn, L.S., Terenzini, P.T. (1996). Influences on students' openness to diversity and challenge in the first year of college. *Journal of Higher Education, 67,* 174-195.

Pascarella, E.T., Edison, M.I., Whitt, E.J., Nora, A., Hagedorn, L.S., & Terenzini, P.T. (1996). Cognitive effects of Greek affiliation during the first year of college. *NASPA Journal, 33,* 242-259.

Pascarella, E.T., & Terenzini, P.T. (1980a). Student-faculty and student-peer relationships as mediators of the structural effects of undergraduate residence arrangement. *Journal of Educational Research, 73,* 344-353.

Pascarella, E.T., & Terenzini, P.T. (1980b). Predicting freshman persistence and voluntary dropout decisions from a theoretical model. *Journal of Higher Education, 51,* 60-75.

Pascarella, E.T., & Terenzini, P.T. (1983). Predicting voluntary freshman year persistence/withdrawal behavior in a residential university: A path analytic validation of Tint's model. *Journal of Educational Psychology, 75,* 215-226.

Pascarella, E.T., & Terenzini, P.T. (1991). *How college affects students.* San Francisco: Jossey-Bass.

Pascarella, E.T., & Terenzini, P.T. (1998). Studying college students in the 21st century: Meeting new challenges. *Review of Higher Education, 21,* 151-156.

Pascarella, E.T., Terenzini, P.T., & Wolfle, L. (1986). Orientation to college and freshman year persistence/withdrawal decisions. *Journal of Higher Education, 57,* 155-175.

Pascarella, E.T., Truckenmiller, R. Nora, A., Terenzini, P.T., Edison, M.I., & Hagedorn, L. S. (in press). Cognitive impacts of intercollegiate athletic participation: Some further evidence. *Journal of Higher Education.*

Pascarella, E.T., Whitt, E.J., Edison, M.I., Nora, A., Hagedorn, L.S., Yeager, P.M., & Terenzini, P.T. (1997). Women's perceptions of a "chilly climate" and their cognitive outcomes during the first year of college. *Journal of College Student Development, 38,* 109-124.

Pascarella, E.T., Whitt, E.J., Nora, A., Edison, M., Hagedorn, L.S., & Terenzini, P.T. (1996). What have we learned from the first year of the National Study of Student Learning? *Journal of College Student Development, 37,* 182-192.

Pew Roundtable (1993). A transatlantic dialogue. *Policy Perspectives, 5 (1),* A1-11.

Phelps, R.E., Altschul, D.B., Wisenbaker, J.M., Slavich, R., Day, J.F., Cooper, D., & Potter, C.G. (1998). Roommate satisfaction and ethnic identity in mixed-race and white university roommate dyads. *Journal of College Student Development, 39,* 194-204.

Pike, G.R., Schroeder, C.C., & Berry, T.R. (1997). Enhancing the educational impact of residence halls: The relationship between residential learning communities and first-year college experiences and persistence. *Journal of College Student Development, 38,* 609-621.

Plato, K. (1978). The shift to student affairs: An analysis of the pattern of change. *NASPA Journal, 15,* 32-36.

Poindexter-Cameron, J.M., & Robinson, T.L. (1997). Relationships among racial identity attitudes, womanist identity attitudes, and self-esteem in African American college women. *Journal of College Student Development, 38,* 288-298.

Rendon, L.I. (1996). Life on the border. *About Campus, 1*(5), 14-20.

Rendon, L.I. (1998). Helping nontraditional students be successful in college. *About Campus, 3*(1), 2-3.

Rhoads, R.A. (1994). *Coming out in college: The struggle for queer identity.* Westport, CT: Bergin & Garvey.

Rhoads, R.A. (1995a). Whales tales, dog piles, and beer goggles: An ethnographic case study of fraternity life. *Anthropology of Education Quarterly, 26*(3), 1-18.

Rhoads, R.A. (1995b). Learning from the coming out experiences of college males. *Journal of College Student Development, 36,* 67-74.

Rhoads, R.A. (1997). Interpreting identity politics: The educational challenge of contemporary student activism. *Journal of College Student Development, 38,* 508-519.

Roberts, S. (1993). *Who we are: A portrait of America.* New York: Times Books.

Romano, C.R. (1996). A qualitative study of women student leaders. *Journal of College Student Development, 37,* 676-683.

Rose, M. (1989). *Lives on the boundary: The struggles and achievements of America's underprepared.* New York: Free Press.

Rudolph, F. (1962). *The American college and university.* New York: Random House.

Schlossberg, N.K., Lynch, A. Q., & Chickering, A.W. (1989). *Improving higher education environments for adults.* San Francisco: Jossey-Bass.

Schroeder, C.C. (1996). Focus on student learning: An imperative for student affairs. *Journal of College Student Development, 37,* 115-117.

Schroeder, C.C., & Hurst, J.C. (1996). Designing learning environments that integrate curricular and cocurricular experiences. *Journal of College Student Development, 37,* 174-181.

Schuh, J.H. (1993). Fiscal pressures on higher education and student affairs. In M.J. Barr & Associates, *The handbook of student affairs administration* (pp. 49-68). San Francisco: Jossey Bass Publishers.

Schwitzer, A.M. (1997). Supporting student learning from a distance. *About Campus, 2(3),* 27-29.

Senge, P.M., (1990). *The fifth discipline: The art and practice of the learning organization.* New York: Doubleday.

Stamatakos, L.C., & Rogers, R. (1984). Student affairs: A profession in need of a philosophy. *Journal of College Student Personnel, 25,* 400-411.

Study Group on Conditions of Excellence in Higher Education (1984). *Involvement in learning: Realizing the potential of American higher education.* Washington, DC: National Institute of Education.

Terenzini, P.T. (1989). Assessment with open eyes: Pitfalls in studying student outcomes. *Journal of Higher Education, 60,* 644-664.

Terenzini, P.T., Pascarella, E.T., & Blimling, G.S. (1996). Students' out-of-class experiences and their influence on cognitive development: A literature review. *Journal of College Student Development, 37,* 149-162.

Terenzini, P.T., Springer, L., Pascarella, E.T., & Nora, A. (1995). Academic and out-of-class influences on students' intellectual orientation. *Review of Higher Education, 19,* 23-44.

Terenzini, P.T., & Upcraft, M. (1996a). Using quantitative methods. In M.L. Upcraft & J.H. Schuh (Eds.), *Assessment in student affairs* (pp. 84-109). San Francisco: Jossey-Bass.

Terenzini, P.T., & Upcraft, M. (1996b). Assessing program and service outcomes. In M.L. Upcraft & J.H. Schuh (Eds.), *Assessment in student affairs* (pp. 217-239). San Francisco: Jossey-Bass.

Tinto, V. (1993). *Leaving college: Rethinking the causes and cures of student attrition. (2nd ed.).* Chicago: University of Chicago Press.

Tinto, V. (1997). Universities as learning organizations. *About Campus, 1(6),* 2-4.

Tinto, V., & Goodsell, A. (1993, April). *Freshman interest groups and the first-year experience: Constructing student communities in a large university.* Paper presented at the annual meeting of the College Reading and Learning Association, Kansas City, MO.

Tinto, V., Goodsell-Love, A., & Russo, P. (1993). Building community. *Liberal Education, 79,* 15-21.

Topper, M.D. (1994). Student loans, debt burdens, and choice of major. In D.H. Finifter, and A.M. Hauptman (Eds.), *America's investment in liberal education.* New Directions For Higher Education, No. 85. San Francisco: Jossey-Bass.

Trow, M. (1970). Elite and popular functions in American Higher Education. In W.R. Niblett (Ed.), *Higher education: Demand and response.* San Francisco: Jossey-Bass.

Upcraft, M.L., & Schuh, J.H. (1996). *Assessment in student affairs: A guide for practitioners*. San Francisco: Jossey-Bass.

Vesey, L.R. (1965). *The emergence of the American university*. Chicago: University of Chicago Press.

Wechsler, H. (1996). Alcohol and the American college campus: A report from the Harvard School of Public Health, *Change*, 20-60.

Wechsler, H. (1997). Facing up to our campus drinking problem: What we know. *About Campus, 2(2)*, 4-8.

Weick, K.E. (1979). *The social psychology of organizing*. Reading, MA: Addison-Wesley.

Weitzer, W.H., & Malaney, G.D. (1991). Of puzzles and pieces: Organizing and directing a campus-based research agenda. In K.J. Beeler & D.E. Hunter (Eds.), *Puzzles and pieces in wonderland: The promise and practice of student affairs research* (pp. 35-54). Washington, DC: National Association of Student Personnel Administrators.

Whitt, E.J. (1994). "I can be anything!": Student leadership at three women's colleges. *Journal of College Student Development, 35*, 198-207.

Whitt, E.J. (1996a). Some propositions worth debating. *About Campus, 1(4)*, 31-32.

Whitt, E.J. (1996b). Assessing student cultures. In M.L. Upcraft & J.H. Schuh (Eds.), *Assessment in student affairs* (pp. 189-216). San Francisco: Jossey-Bass.

Whitt, E.J., Carnaghi, J.E., Matkin, J., Love, P.G., & Nestor, D. (1990). Believing is seeing: Alternative perspectives on a statement of professional philosophy for student affairs. *NASPA Journal, 27*, 178-184.

Whitt, E.J., Edison, M.I., Pascarella, E.T., Nora, A., & Terenzini, P.T. (1999a). Interactions with peers and objective and self-reported cognitive outcomes across three years of college. *Journal of College Student Development, 40*, 61-78.

Whitt, E.J., Edison, M.I., Pascarella, E.T., Nora, A., & Terenzini, P.T. (1999b). Women's perceptions of a "chilly climate" and cognitive outcomes in college: Additional evidence. *Journal of College Student Development, 40,* 163-177.

Whitt, E.J., & Pascarella, E.T. (1999). Using systematic inquiry to improve performance. In G.S. Blimling, E.J. Whitt, & Associates, *Good practice in student affairs: Principles to foster student learning* (pp.91-112). San Francisco: Jossey-Bass.

Williams, L.B. (1997). Telling tales in school. *About Campus, 2(2),* 2-3.

Williams, L.B. (1998). Behind every face is a story. *About Campus, 3(1),* 16-21.

Willimon, W.H. (1997). Has higher education abandoned its students? *About Campus, 2(4),* 4-9.

Willimon, W.H., & Willimon, W.P. (1998). On college and friendship. *About Campus, 3(2),*11-15.

Wingspread Group on Higher Education (1993). *An American imperative: Higher expectations for higher education.* Racine, WI: The Johnson Foundation.

Young, R.B. (1996). Guiding values and philosophy. In S.R Komives and D.B. Woodard (Eds.), *Student services: A handbook for the profession.* (3d ed.) (pp. 83-105). San Francisco: Jossey-Bass.

To order more copies of this publication or to find out about other titles offered by NASPA, please contact NASPA at www.naspa.org or 202-265-7500.